Thirty Walks of the
Wild Atlantic Way
Cork, Kerry and Clare

by Damien Enright

Published by **Maps N' Charts Ltd.**

ISBN 978-1-78280-780-3

Text and photography: Damien Enright

Loop Head, Slieve Elva, Black Head and Abbey Hill walks: Fintan Enright MA Lit

Design, maps and illustration: Matthew Enright

Maps N' Charts Ltd.
Derryconnell (L8446)
Schull, Skibbereen, Co. Cork P81 TP66, Ireland

t: +353 (0)28 37370   f: +353 (0)28 37660
m: +353 (0)87 251 7452   e: mizen@eircom.net

ATLANTIC OCEAN

KERRY

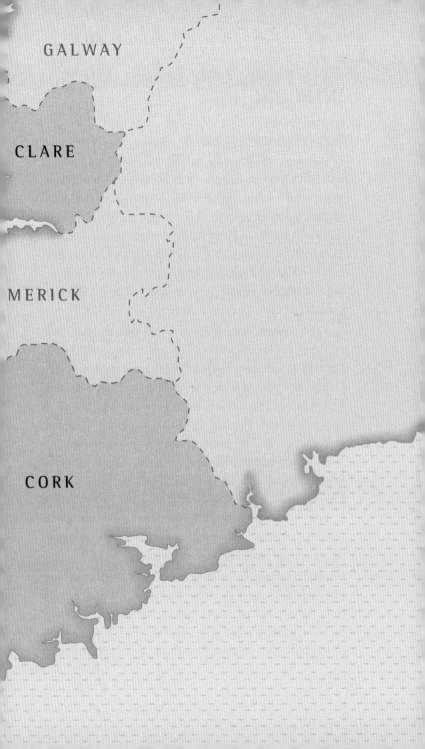

INTRODUCTION

The Wild Atlantic Way extends 2,500km along the wave-beaten western coasts of Ireland. In writing a guide to walks which might be enjoyed as a diversion while driving this dramatic route, I have begun at the town of Kinsale. Motorists coming from southern Britain and the Continent are likely to arrive in Ringaskiddy, Co Cork, only 25km from Kinsale, or in Rosslare Port, to which Kinsale is the nearest point on Wild Atlantic Way itinerary. Beginning at Kinsale, the visitor's first experience of Ireland will be the Munster counties of Cork, Kerry and Clare.

I would suggest that while the Wild Atlantic Way route provides the opportunity to see and enjoy 2,500 km of Ireland's magnificent coastline from a car, rubber on the tarmac does not provide the same insights into Ireland, its landscape and culture, as do boots on the ground. A concern, shared with Mr. Ciarán O'Carroll, my publisher, that the rewards of open-air encounters with the land and its people might go unappreciated, prompted me to write this book. It is my wish, and, likely the wish of every Irishman and woman, that our visitors pause in their travels to take in those particular features that make our island unique, in addition to enjoying the sweeping, stunning seascapes and landscapes viewed from the car.

It is also a principle of mine that the boots should not have to travel far in order to enjoy the Ireland not experienced from the car. Indeed, boots, per se, will not be necessary, on most walks sensible shoes will do. This is not a book of treks or route marches. The itineraries are, for the most part, gentle perambulations during which the walker will have time to stop and stare, to take in the fine points of our rich and (largely) unspoiled natural history, the forms, fragrances and hues of the Irish countryside. They will present opportunities to see at close quarters the daily round of urban and rural life, to explore the byways, churches and monuments of ancient towns, the prehistory of dolmens, barrow graves and megaliths, the land itself and its crops and husbandry.

Pastoral scenes may well be met and savoured – a herd of cows meandering home for milking in the evening, wide-eyed young calves with earrings (actually identification tags) staring at one over gate bars, skittish half-wild mountain sheep on hillside roads. Such encounters, close-up and personal for the foot traveller, distinguish our country from others. And, it is to be remembered that, out walking, one will meet people; and the Irish, in general, like to talk. They are proud of their country, and happy to explain it and share it. "When God made Time, he made plenty of it", there is no rush to move on. In walking the Cork, Kerry and Clare routes outlined in these pages, the reader will, I hope, not only enjoy the lilt of the landscape, but become a moving part of it.

CONTENTS

CORK WALKS FROM KINSALE WEST

KERRY WALKS FROM BUNAW TO SHANNON ESTUARY

CLARE KILRUSH TO BALLYVAGHAN

* Worthwhile walks a short distance inland from the
  Wild Atlantic Way.

While every effort has been made to ensure that the
contents of this publication are correct at the time of going
to press, no liability can be accepted for trespass, accident
or loss of life by the public in walking these routes.
Care should be taken on all roadways.

CORK WILD ATLANTIC WAY WALKS
FROM KINSALE WEST

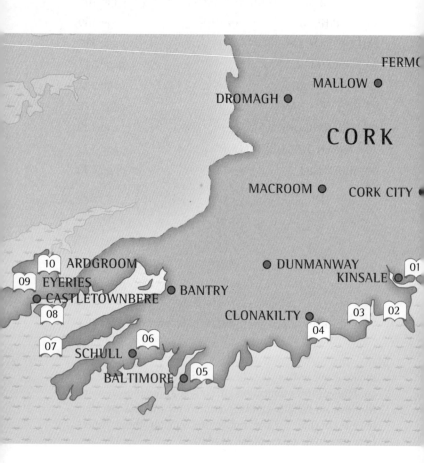

FERMO

MALLOW ○

DROMAGH ○

CORK

MACROOM ○   CORK CITY ●

10 ARDGROOM   ○ DUNMANWAY   01
09 EYERIES   KINSALE ●
○ CASTLETOWNBERE   ○ BANTRY
08   CLONAKILTY ○   03   02
                                        04
07   06
SCHULL ○
BALTIMORE ○   05

KINSALE TOWN AND COUNTRY WALK

Distance and Time: 4km, 2hrs.

Difficulty: Easy. Pavements and quiet roads. A gentle climb for a quarter of a mile. Comfortable shoes are quite adequate for this walk, all on pavements or tarred by-roads.

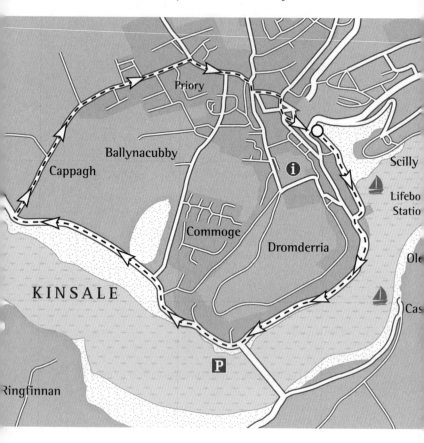

GETTING THERE:

Our starting point on the Wild Atlantic Way is Kinsale. Ahead of us, we have miles of spectacular coastline, colourful villages, romantic ruins, towns with fine architecture and great houses, and well- preserved monuments of Ireland's prehistoric culture. But before setting out, we should explore Kinsale town, emblematic in Irish history. It was at Kinsale that the fate of the Irish was decided in a tragic battle. Here, the old Gaelic order was lost forever, and our chieftains, 'The Wild Geese', forced into exile. We start our tour of this fascinating town at the Tourist Office in the town centre, with a large public car park alongside.

Kinsale: a pavement-side memorial to the mass grave of victims of The Great Famine.

THE WALK:

Stepping out of the Tourist Office, we set off to the left, along the waterfront. Opposite, across the Inner Harbour, is the salient of Scilly, with its imposing old buildings on the shore. The road along which we walk was built in the last century. Before then, the area to our right was under water, with knuckles of quays protruding into the harbour at right angles. In the 17th century, and again in the 19th century, Kinsale was an important fishing port. For the spring mackerel season, fleets of boats from Cornwall and the Isle of Man assembled, and fish, salted or packed in ice brought from Norway, was shipped to the English markets.

At the Trident Hotel, we reach World's End, as it is called locally, said to have been thus named by Viking longshipmen wintering there, far from home. We follow the pavement west along the water.

Passing the bridge, we continue along the water, past the car park and quarry. The Bandon here is a fine, broad river, once a thoroughfare for boats delivering goods to the small quays along its banks. We shortly come to Commoge Marsh on the right. Painted plaques illustrate the bird species, many of which fly phenomenal distances to reach here, including godwits from Iceland, and knot, from the Canadian High Arctic.

Cappagh Lane, 200 yards beyond the creek, is almost hidden. On the sharp bend after the marsh, it, and a laneway to a house, leave the road as one. As we ascend the lane, views over the marsh, river and harbour are available but it is worth waiting for the spectacular view from the top. Having contemplated it, we retrace our steps to the road, continuing until we turn right at the T-junction and descend towards the town.

St. Multose Church, Kinsale – straight out of medieval Normandy.

Downhill, downhill, the town's roofscapes and steeples appearing below, and when we see a line of toytown cottages on our right we turn sharp left, uphill, and take the first right into Lower Catholic Walk. This leads us to the Carmelite Friary church, an impressive building. The Carmelite Order has been associated with Kinsale almost continuously since 1334.

The tree-lined avenue that leads downhill from the front door of the church is somewhat reminiscent of a small 'ramblas' in a Spanish town. At the end, we turn right, into Cork Street, and immediately notice Desmond Castle, a Custom House built in the 16th century by the Earls of Desmond and later used as a prison for French sailors when England was at war with Napoleon.

Past Desmond Castle, in the same street, the imposing church of St. John the Baptist stands. The left turning opposite takes us to Church Street, where we turn left again, passing in front of Kinsale's most famous building, St. Multose Church.

St Multose is immediately arresting in its appearance. Straight out of medieval Normandy, it is quite unlike the ancient churches we are familiar with in Ireland. It reminds us, more than other Norman ruins, of the 'Frenchness' of these invaders when they first came. It was built circa 1195, by Milo de Cogan, and designed like the stolid country churches of Northern France. It has a second unique distinction; it has been a place of worship for an unbroken eight hundred years.

We continue left along Church Street, and cross the junction into Market Place and Market Square. A stroll down Market Quay returns us to our trailhead.

A teal drake, small and brightly plumaged, common in
Kinsale Bay.

GARRETSTOWN WOODS AND ANCIENT DEER WALL WALK

Distance and Time: Coillte forest paths, 4km.
Approx. 1.5hrs.

Difficulty: Easy forest paths, one medium steep downhill stretch. An opportunity to see a wide variety of Ireland's wild flowers in spring.

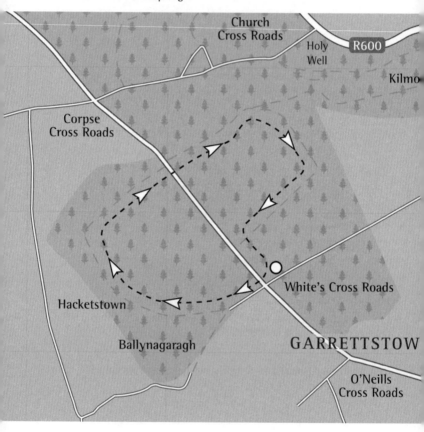

GETTING THERE:

On the R600 going west from Kinsale town, the Wild Atlantic Way takes us to the spectacular Old Head of Kinsale, via the R604 and L3233. Returning on the L3233, we pass Garretstown Strand and keep left on the R604. Soon after the forest begins, we reach a green triangle on the right, with a plinth supporting three milk churns. This is White's Cross, our trailhead.

THE WALK:

We cross the road from the milk churn monument, and set off on the unpaved track leading past a new, stone-fronted house on the right, to the forest entrance, ahead.

The milk churns are 'iconic'. Once a common sight at cross-roads, they recall the days of the milk lorries initiated by the local cooperative creameries. Started in the late 19th century, the creameries greatly improved the economic lot of Irish farmers, evolving into agricultural societies processing milk into butter, cooperatively purchasing seed and agricultural equipment and making short-term credit available.

From the seventeenth century, salted, hand-churned butter was exported in firkins from the butter markets in Cork, Waterford and Limerick. Up to the 1960s, lorries from local creameries did a daily round to collect milk left in churns by farmers at selected cross-roads. The lorries were mobile mini-creameries, carrying equipment for weighing and separating the milk. After Ireland joined the EEC in 1973, smaller creameries were closed or merged with others to form larger co-ops.

The track takes us to a 'barber pole' barrier. When tree felling is in progress, warning signs, or Keep Out signs, may be in place. However, such activities are only occasional. The forestry road ahead is surfaced with large, stone chips. The route becomes more sylvan as we walk, with forests on either side. The trees are Sitka spruce; note the smooth, grey bark which peels off in disc-like plates. Since their introduction to Britain and Ireland, they have become the most extensively planted commercial tree. They grow quickly, thrive on many soil types and deliver large quantities of excellent timber per hectare. Resistant to disease, they are also unattractive to deer and voles, which attack other conifers. Requiring abundant moisture, they flourish in our climate, and in western and northern Britain where conditions in their native American habitat are also replicated; the name comes from Sitka Sound in Alaska.

When the forest thins, the path side supports goat willow, rhododendron, briars and wildflowers. Just beyond, are plantations of young spruce. When the rhododendron is in flower, a spectacular display edges the track on the right before we reach a barrier where we cross the quiet public road. Opposite, we pass through another forestry barrier and enter a track rising gently between young conifer plantations. In spring and summer, wildflowers are abundant. The cushions of golden trefoil and purple-flowered foxgloves are the most striking, but look out for tiny yellow pimpernels and bright blue germander speedwell half hidden in the grass.

After the forestry road tops a low rise and begins to descend, we reach a waymark post on the left. Opposite it, on our right, is a narrow, foot worn path ascending slightly. When walking it, notice the overgrown wall on the right, with 'spears' of sharp stones protruding. At the end of this wall, as the path turns right, and then left, we reach an 'interpretation post' from which a Perspex information plaque swings out like a railway signal. This tells us that the wall was built circa 1750 and the purpose of the protruding stones was to prevent deer from jumping it and reaching the crop fields beyond.

As the path veers left, the forest is tall, dark and sombre, but thinned by tree fellings. The footpath soon becomes a forest track between high conifers. It leads us to a barrier beyond which is the public road. Turning left, we are shortly back at our trailhead.

The mile-long storm beaches at Garretstown are a favourite haunt of surfers in rough weather.

TIMOLEAGUE ABBEY AND VILLAGE WALK

Distance and Time: 7.2km, including viewing the abbey and the Church of Ireland, 2-3hrs.

Difficulty: Secondary roads with few cars.
Two medium steep stretches.

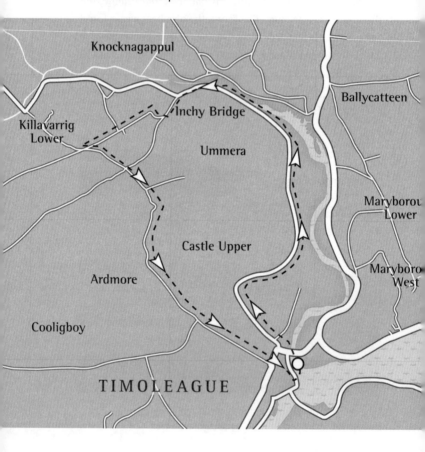

GETTING THERE:

Timoleague village is on the Wild Atlantic Way about 45 minutes west of Kinsale. We see its large ruined abbey as we approach, and we park in front of it where there are picnic tables facing Courtmacsherry Bay. A wealth of bird life may be seen foraging or roosting in the shallows or on the mudbanks. Gracious Timoleague house is just upriver from the bridge which we have crossed before parking.

Timoleague Abbey, one of Ireland's great monasteries, founded 1240, burnt by English soldiers 1612.

THE WALK:

Timoleague Abbey was established on the site of a monastery founded by Saint Molaga, a holy man who devoted himself to the care of plague victims in the 7th century. Tig Molaga means the House of Molaga. The Annals of the Four Masters record that the foundations of the present abbey were laid by a McCarthy chieftain in 1240, the site having been a place of pilgrimage since Molaga's time.

Before Bandon town had been established by Richard Boyle, Earl of Cork, Timoleague was a bustling commercial centre. Quays and hostelries burgeoned with Spanish and French merchants. The friars conducted a thriving trade in wine.

Facing the bay, we cross the road and go left along the grass verge toward the bridge spanning the River Argideen. Looking up-river, we are presented with a classic view of Timoleague House and castle.

We go left and follow the wall enclosing Timoleague Church of Ireland and graveyard, entered around the corner to the right. The interior of the church is unique and resembles more a corner of the Taj Mahal than an Irish village chapel interior. Craftsmen sent from India by the Maharajah of Gwalior created the work as a memorial to his physician, Lieut. Col. Crofts of the Indian Medical Service who had saved his son's life, and whose parish church was Timoleague.

Leaving the church grounds, we turn right and pass the gates of Timoleague House as we set off out of the village. We shortly pass the imposing RC Church on the left. A west-facing window is the work of an Irish stained glass master, Harry Clark.

We are soon walking above the western bank of the Argideen. After passing through tunnels of trees, where wood anemones grow in spring and wood blewits and parasol mushrooms in winter, we come to Inchy Bridge. The Argideen is one of Munster's most famous sea trout and salmonoid rivers. Bats flit over the pool below us on summer nights, including Daubenton's, the water bat. Kingfishers are often seen. Dippers, small birds that walk under the water to hunt for small fish and caddis are often seen.

Timoleague House, seat of the Travers family, beside the beautiful River Argideen.

We do not cross the bridge, but continue ahead to a branch of the Barryroe Coop. Ballinascarthy and Clonakilty are signposted. We bear left, past a house with many-headed cordyline palms. Shortly, a road goes off to our left but, continuing to the right, we reach a typical country road taking us to Killavarrig Cross Roads. Here, we go left, doubling back and climbing up the hill. The ascent is steep but we get panoramic views of the lovely country to the west and north.

We pass through a crossroads. Now, on these high lands, we can see for miles. At a brake of gorse, and a gurgling stream, a 'dog leg' turning takes us up another short steep climb. We reach the summit at Ardmore and descend towards Timoleague village. Immediately, we have a magnificent view of Courtmacsherry Bay. When the tide is out, vast mudflats are exposed, supporting up to 20,000 birds that migrate to overwinter there, feeding on the rich throve of invertebrates.

Our descent is steep, and soon the Abbey, our trailhead, and the painted houses of Timoleague appear. Lemon yellow, sky blue, rose red and pastel green, it is clear that the Timoleague people are, indeed, fearless with paint!

PS. A suggestion. The next town on the Wild Atlantic Way is Clonakilty. An alternative route to reach there (marked Coastal Route) is to cross the bridge in front of the abbey, take the road down the bay to picturesque Courtmacsherry and then follow the coast, via the spectacular Seven Heads, to Ring village on Clonakilty Bay.

Timoleague Church of Ireland. Giant yew trees in the graveyard, mosaics like the Taj Mahal inside.

INCHYDONEY ISLAND WALK

Distance and Time: 6.5km, 1.5hrs.

Difficulty: An easy walk, sand beach, shoreline path, (some of the rocks may be slippery), road, cross-country trail and dunes. This is a favourite walk of mine for birdwatching in winter.

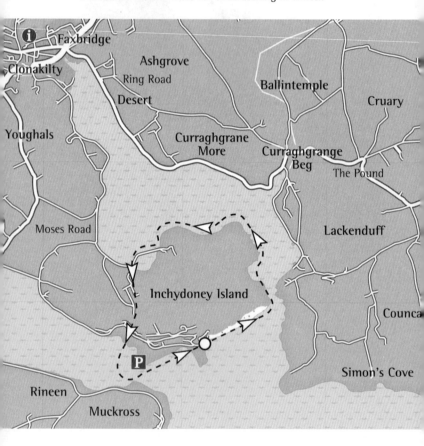

GETTING THERE:

At the rounabout entering Clonakilty from Timoleague on the Wild Atlantic Way, we take the second exit — the bypass around the town — and then the first left, signposted "Model Railway Village" and "Inchydoney Beach". As we arrive above the beach, and pass summer cottages, the road becomes one-way and takes us directly to the car park in front of the hotel. The walk starts from here.

THE WALK:

Leaving the public car park, we pass the hotel on our left and, turning our backs on it, descend steep steps to the eastern strand. Beyond the enormous hotel are miles of sand as wild and beautiful as any in west Cork. Ahead, a kilometre away, is Ring Channel, with green hillsides beyond.

The beach is backed by dunes, colonised by marram grass. The surf rolls in and sea birds cry overhead. Dunlin or sanderling may be seen skittering along the waterline, busy little birds rushing in and out of the sea. Oystercatcher will also be seen with their red beaks, red legs and neat black-and-white plumage.

Long-term home to an enterprising non-conformist, this substantial craft is a feature of the walk along Ring Channel.

Where the beach ends, we follow the shore to the left or, at high tide, cross the dunes. Banded snails are common and, in summer, black-and-red burnet moths, or cinnabar moths with their black-and-amber caterpillars. Now, as we walk between the dunes and Ring channel, Ring village comes into view opposite, a pretty pier with boats, and another pier, nearer the open sea, below it.

The water's edge is often busy with black-tailed godwits, curlew, whimbrel, redshank, turnstones, oystercatchers, cormorants, shelduck, merganser, egrets, herons, swans, sometimes Brent geese; any or all are present in winter.

The rough path following the channel toward the bay head and Clonakilty town nurtures seaweeds of diverse hues and species (but slippery at times!) and is splashed with lichens yellow as eggs yolks, green as jade and even pink as pomegranates. Sea-ivory, a hard, crinkly lichen, aka Neptune's Beard, grows on the stone walls on the left.

We pass a wide-bellied moored boat, the solitary and singular home of one of the many west Cork blow-ins who seek to live a quieter life. Here, on the island's undeveloped side, it is removed from the palatial hotel where Bertie Ahern, Ray Burke and the Fianna Fail crew posed during their annual self-congratulation fests. Unfortunately, on winter evenings, the lights of Clonakilty glare in the sky 3km away at the bay-head.

At the end of the channel-side path, we reach the tarred road that runs between the bay and Beamish's Lagoon, as the lake on our left is called. Swans drift on the surface and the willows at the far end provide nesting sites for egrets, the pretty, stork-like birds lately naturalised in Ireland. Where it ends, facing a cottage, we turn left up a leafy road fringed with tall bulrushes. We pass a mossy ruin and then high stone walls sheltering a nuns' retreat.

Passing through a hill-top stile, we head down onto Muckross Strand. On winter evenings, the channel-edge toward Clonakilty town is carpeted with migrant flocks. We walk left and, rounding the corner of the dunes, continue onto Inchydoney main beach, with surfers, black as seals, out on the waves, or holidaymakers on their coloured towels on summer days.

A ten-minute stroll along the beach and a flight of steps return us to the car park. Warmth and Christmas cheer will be available in the hotel but, if the evening is right, we might pause to watch the sun gild the mirror-calm channel to the west.

Ring village. Colourful houses reflected in the still water,
a small pier, some boats.

SKIBBEREEN/BALTIMORE: LOUGH HYNE WALK

Distance and Time: 6km, 2hrs.

Difficulty: Byroads. One steep climb. Options -
follow additional hillside and woodland paths.

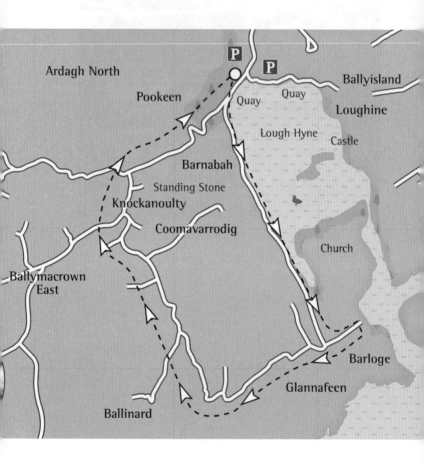

GETTING THERE:

Lough Hyne, a unique phenomenon recognised and studied by marine biologist from all over the world, remains as tranquil and lovely in its surroundings as an inland lake. It is highly recommended as an opportunity for a two - hour stroll just off the R595 spur of the Wild Atlantic Way south of Skibbereen.

At Skibereen, the R595 is signposted Baltimore/ Lough Hyne. 3km beyond Skibbereen, go left on L4207 (sign for Skibbereen Golf Club nearby). After 3km. we reach the lake. Our trailhead is the parking space under trees on the right. Interpretation boards along the shore detail the elements that created this enormous, unique rock pool and illustrate various creatures that inhabit it.

THE WALK:

Lough Hyne was Europe's first Marine Nature Reserve. The tides filling the lake twice a day create a habitat of relatively warm, well-oxygenated water supporting a great diversity of marine plants and animals including seventy two fish species. Scientists come from all over the world to study its unique environment.

To scuba dive beneath Lough Hyne's waters would be a truly remarkable experience; we, however, must be content with exploring the singular landscape that surrounds it. The adventurous may climb a hill to overlook the famous tidal race.

We set out along the lake shore, keeping the water beside us on our left. The scenery is immediately beautiful, with beech trees ahead and gorse and bracken on the slopes across the water. Even in winter, these slopes are colourful, the red bracken and white rock outcrops reflected on the lake waters.

In spring, gorse and wild daffodils, then bluebells and sea pinks will be in bloom, and in autumn, the deciduous trees along the way are dressed in all their burnished glory.

We pass a small pier, a quaint tin house opposite. Offshore, the water is some 40m deep. Nearby, Japanese knotweed and winter heliotrope have become established but are kept in check. At lake centre, we see Cloghan Island. When the trees are leafless, the ruins of Cloghan Castle, once an O'Driscoll tower house, are visible. The creek on our left does not connect with the sea, but is pretty when boats are moored on its still waters and the slopes above are carpeted in red bracken, with stone walls and rock faces brilliant in the sun.

We pass the occasional house, and go left down a tree-lined road to the main pier, the base for lake exploration. To our right is Bulloch Island, rising from sheer cliffs. The entrance of the tide-race to the lough is to our left and, as an option, we can reach the high ground above it by first clambering along the rocky shore and, after some 150m, taking a path up a green valley which leads us to the heights. The come-and-go of the tide is spectacular, the water racing in against the outflow or out against the inflow, great kelp forests moving in the direction of the prevailing current. Stasis briefly results from this 'conflict of the waters'; the cataracts are momentarily in equilibrium; all is uncannily still.

Returning to the lake circuit, we go straight ahead, uphill, a steepish climb up to Barloge Hill. After the route goes right, and levels, look out for a ringfort in a field on the left. From this 'plateau', the vista is magnificent, a panorama broadening with every step. Before us is Roaring Water Bay, its islands and Mount Gabriel with its twin 'golf ball' tracking stations, and far behind, northwards, the mountains of Beara, Slieve Miskish and the western Cahas. We see the islands west to Cape Clear and east to Ringarogy. All is especially beautiful in the evening, under the western sun.

Reaching two T-junctions in quick succession, we go right at each, walking steeply downhill, the lake coming into view. Steps lead upward to Knockomagh Wood, an option which will also take us back to our trailhead.

Tireless walkers may now continue on a there-and-back walk along the lakeshore road, the water on their right. They will reach a pretty pier with interpretation boards and a grassy salient fringed with white scurvy grass and pink sea thrift in season.

The still, salt waters of Lough Hyne, a marine phenomenon much studied by biologists, cut off by hills blanketed in bracken, gorse and heather from the sea.

LETTER AND BARNANCLEEVE WALK

Distance and Time: 8km, 2-3hrs.

Difficulty: Possibly muddy in winter. A short gradient; no steep climbs

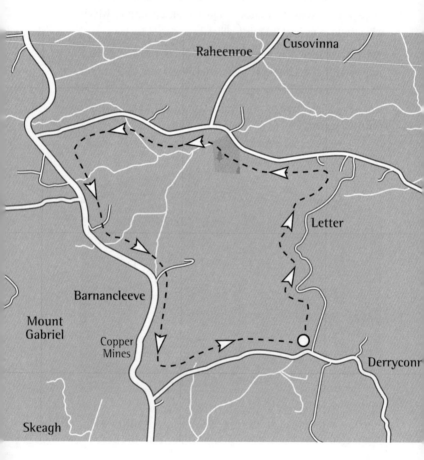

GETTING THERE:

After Ballydehob, the Wild Atlantic Way becomes the R592. The land on both sides of the road is often wild and bockety, up and down like a jig, with breaks of furze and heather, and distant hills across expansive bog land. A short distance up a byroad beyond Ballydehob, a fine walk takes us below Mount Gabriel into the tranquillity and silence of these low hills, and opens to a spectacular view over Roaringwater Bay and its many islands. To reach it, we turn right (north) approx. 4km beyond Ballydehob onto the L8446, a small road signposted "Derryconnell House". The road veers sharp left soon after the Derryconnell entrance. We ignore the lane to the right, continue 300m beyond it to a small cottage on the right and we park nearby. This is our trailhead. A gate on the right opens to a green track to the hills.

THE WALK:

The gate at the entrance of the green road for Letter – 'leitir' meaning 'wet hillside' – is the first of three gates on this route. Care should be taken to ensure that they are left as found; cattle and sheep graze the rough land in between. Also, walkers should not take dogs, and take care to avoid contact with livestock.

As we walk between the flat fields of rough grazing, the silence is immediately noticeable. We soon cross a brown stream at another gate. The path swings left and then right and climbs gently. Roaring Water Bay and Cape Clear Island can now be seen behind us.

We reach the highest point of the green road. Ahead of us, the land falls away and, to the north-west, we see the high mountains of Kerry beyond Dunmanus and even beyond Bantry Bay. There are ruins of long-abandoned stone houses on the left, and a copse of trees ahead. We arrive at the third and last gate, a formidable barrier where a stile would be much appreciated by the walker.

On our right we pass a large, neat farmhouse and, to the left, old buildings, their stone walls beautifully patterned with lichens. Now, the road is paved and we pass three colourful whitewashed out-houses, with red oxide painted doors and tin roofs.

At the end of the lane, we reach a narrow tarred road and turn left. Some minutes farther on, on our left, we pass the cottage of the respected poet, John Montague, more often teaching at American universities than at home. It is certainly a poetic location, with peace in abundance and wild, stark scenery. Montague's lines, in his poem 'King & Queen', "...band after band/ of terminal,/ peewit haunted/ cropless bogland." might well have been written about this landscape.

We are now walking due west; Mount Gabriel is, at times, dead ahead. We ignore a road to the right. Bogland is to our left and, sometimes, also to our right. The road is straight, and treeless.

Arriving at a T-junction, at the main Schull-Durrus road, we turn left, walking south, climbing gently towards the gap at Barnancleeve. Fuchsia bushes line the verge here and there as the road continues to rise gently, giving wider and wider views.

We pass the entrance to a house on the right and, as we top the rise, come upon a spectacular view. The road clings to the right hand side of the valley beneath the steep escarpment under Mount Gabriel, cutting into the slope. Roaring Water Bay and numerous islands lie spread out below us, an awe-inspiring vista. The largest island in full view is Cape Clear, the smallest – and most dramatic – the distant Fastnet Rock. The rock, with its lighthouse, was the last sight of Ireland for emigrants sailing to America and was known as Ireland's teardrop.

We start downhill, the road ahead seen below us almost all the way to Schull. Far off to our left, part of Baltimore is in view, its beacon visible to the naked eye on clear days, gleaming white in the sun.

Some 700m or so below Barnancleeve gap we see pine trees ahead and a white house with two chimneys. Here, we turn left and, for a kilometre, follow an undulating, lonely road through the fastness of the hills to arrive back at our trailhead.

A old stone-posted gate at the start of the Letter walk, with the wild hills and bogs stretching miles beyond.

TIP OF SHEEP'S HEAD WALK

Distance and Time: 3.5km, 2hrs.

Difficulty: An anticlockwise circuit of the headland's western tip, the Sheep's Hoof, one might call it — it is shaped like a hoof, with Lough Akeen splitting the 'toes'. 3.5km, 2hrs. Good strong boots. Not recommended in wet, misty or stormy weather.

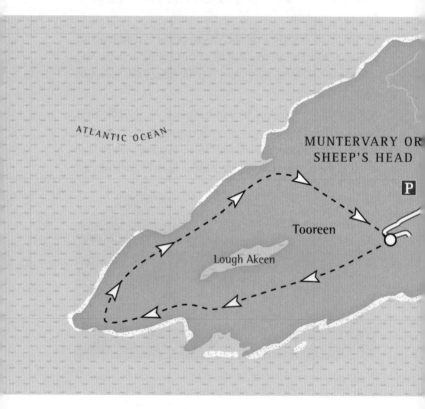

ATLANTIC OCEAN

MUNTERVARY OR
SHEEP'S HEAD

Tooreen

Lough Akeen

GETTING THERE:

To reach the tip of The Sheeps Head peninsula, we follow the Wild Atlantic Way which turns sharply south (left) at Durrus. The road, the L4704 follows Dunmanus Bay through Ahakista and Kilcrohane to our trailhead at Tooreen Turning Point, approx. 8km beyond Kilcrohane.

THE WALK:

The track going west leads us downhill; when it splits, we head for the waymark on the path above. We shortly see Dunmanus Bay and the north tip of Mizen Head. The tracks are rocky. Stepping stones have been installed over wet ground.

Our views of the broad Atlantic and the wild landscape are magnificent. The Sheeps Head is one of Ireland's unique scenic treasures. Where possible, the power lines to the lighthouse should be buried; retaining the unspoiled ruggedness should be a priority.

Sometimes the track passes between ridges and panoramas are temporarily obscured. Near the headland's tip, a short ascent above the path will reveal Lough Akeen directly below. Care should be taken: the location is perfect for a Tarzan-like dive straight down into the black depths, but I imagine most walkers would prefer not to.

Beyond Waymark 252, Bere Island beacon, marking the channel into Bere Haven, is clear to see. The hills behind the Beara mountains continue into Kerry, their soft contours fading into the distance.

At a plateau, we go fairly steeply downhill, Lough Akeen on our right, reeded at the western end. Signs warn about the cliffs nearby. Beyond a footbridge, we see their formidable precipices on our left. The tip of Beara becomes visible and the westernmost end of Dursey Island extending beyond Crow Head.

Below us, the helicopter pad serving the lighthouse is ringed with white-painted stones. A sign points to the lighthouse, an automatic station 82m. above the sea. Its twin stands on Calf Rock off Dursey, opposite. Together, they guide tankers safely into Bantry Bay to the Whiddy Island Oil Storage Depot.

We retrace our steps past the helicopter pad, and descend, left, toward a waymark below. Waymark 242 is in a rocky valley with fallen slabs large enough to offer shelter.

A shallow, kilometre-long gorge follows, with sides sloping to the flat floor as if it had been scoured out; however, glaciation is unlikely to have reached these peninsulas. The lichens on the rocks are cobalt blue, pastel green, cadmium yellow, red and grey. Some are snow-white blobs, like paint. Signs warn us as we pass close to a cliff with drops of 70m into the sea.

Far below, a smooth sea rock, shiny and grey, is like the back of a humpbacked whale. Fulmar glide on the air currents or sit on their nests in grassy niches. Sheep graze on ledges no bigger than hearthrugs, hundreds of feet over the sea. Passing Post 236, we reach a stile and ascend a slope, following the posts. The salient near 235 offers panoramic views over Bantry Bay.

At Post 231, we follow the waymarks steeply uphill to complete the loop: the 'main' track continues east toward Bantry. On the slope, we come to a galvanised gate with a stile and some stepping stones. Eastward stand the gables of a roofless stone house, with overgrown fields marked in front. This is the first indication of settlement. Soon, we pass more rough fields, the stones cleared from them forming the boundary ditches.

A roofless stone ruin, with one small window in the gable stands near the track, once the pathway into this smallholding, climbing alongside walls colonised by saxifrage and ferns. Below, on a ditch, a wind-sculpted tree, a stunted blackthorn, has managed to grow. Shortly, we see the electricity poles again and then, above us, Tooreen Turning Point, our trailhead.

A ruin on the Bantry Bay side of Sheeps Head. Evidence of ancient potato drills can be seen. Ruins abandoned during the Great Famine are common sights in West Cork, where tens of thousands of landless tenant-farmers starved or emigrated.

BERE ISLAND WALK

Distance and Time: 9km, 2.5-3hrs.

Difficulty: Largely gentle terrain, with one steep sector for about 200m on a rough track. Stout shoes or boots are advisable, especially in damp weather.

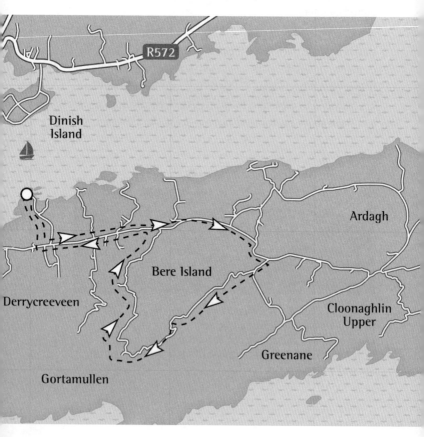

GETTING THERE:

We follow the R572 Wild Atlantic Way to Castletownbere, where we take the ferry to Bere Island. See bereisland.net for ferry timetables.

THE WALK:

Bere Island is close to shore, but it has the same feeling of apartness from the mainland as the further flung islands of West Cork. Looking at it from the sea front of Castletownberehaven, it seems little different in character from the beautiful and rugged coast to east or west but one seems to be entering another world the moment one steps off the ferry.

We begin the walk at the West Pier and set off uphill. Some of the island cars are falling to pieces where they stand and these, along with a couple of wrecked boats, somehow make the scene picturesque and distinctly not 'mainland'.

Arriving at a T-junction, we turn left. Ignoring a crossroads, we continue on the straight road east. We soon cross Ballynakilla Bridge and pass the old school — a site with marvellous views — its yard overgrown with rushes, loosestrife, montbretia, bindweed and a dozen other wildflowers. We ignore the right turning, uphill. Here, we have spectacular views of the Slieve Miskish Mountains across the sound, with Hungry Hill to the right.

* Note that the off-road loop is closed on
  January 31st each year.

Now, as we top a rise on the road, we see a Martello Tower on a bare hill ahead of us. We ignore the left turning marked the Beara Cycle Route; Greenane is signposted, ahead and there is a roadside map of the island. Pines line the road, with occasional large trees, sycamore, with red leaf stems and 'helicopter' seedpods, and ash, with leaves that move in the breeze like feathers. We ignore another left.

At a nest of roadside signs, we head right, uphill, signposted the Standing Stone and the Lighthouse. We shortly reach the Standing Stone, or gallán, on our left, with a plaque telling us that it dates from the Bronze Age 2000 BC to 500 BC. This spot affords magnificent views. On the lower slopes, the hill is hemmed with green. In dry weather, it is brown above, and in mist and rain the wet rocks below the summit gleam like veins of silver set in the grass and bracken of the slope. At the eastern end of Bere another signal tower may be seen and, across Bantry Bay, on the Sheeps Head, small coves, often backed by caves, and the 'nose' of the Sheep extending westward into the Atlantic.

Opposite the Standing Stone, we leave the road and take the hill track. A stile gives access. A cross is visible on the small hill ahead. The higher we go, the better the views, and it is breathtaking to look down on the world below. Shortly after passing the cross, we reach the top of our gentle climb. The scene is now of wild and rugged land, rock and bog, with no sign of humans or human habitation. There are few birds, and these are specialists, rock pipits and ravens, and the occasional "Poor Law" robin. Gulls soar high overhead and a hovering kestrel or a hunting peregrine falcon may be seen.

The path reaches a T-junction, and we go right. We are heading downhill towards the Bere Haven Sound, back to civilisation. Now, to the left, is the continuance of the Beara Way leading to the west end of the island and then back to the pier — this option can be easily followed on the map and adds about 4km. to our walk. We ignore the track and continue on the road. Reaching the dorsal road again at Ballynakilla Bridge, we turn left and then go right, down to the pier, and our trailhead.

A raven, common on these coasts, screams blue murder at a cliff walker venturing too close to its nest site on a ledge above the storm-tossed sea below.

EYERIES, WEST CORK: HAG OF BEARA AND LOUGH FADA WALK

Distance and Time: 15km, allow 4hrs.

Difficulty: Coastal road, steep ascents and descents; can be windy. 3km stretch of moorland trail, muddy in wet weather.

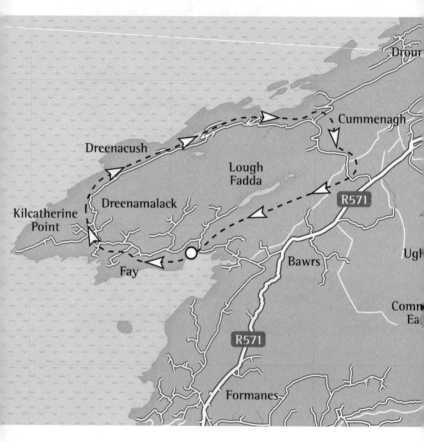

GETTING THERE:

Eyeries village is on R571 Wild Atlantic Way, north from Allihies and Castletownbere. Driving north of the village, passing the church and Post Office, we pick up the Beara Way coast road, and continue 4Km to a signpost, on a broad curve, indicating Lough Fada to the right. Park here, the trailhead.

THE WALK:

The waymarked Beara Way follows the signpost toward Lough Fada. We walk west on the coast road. The views are, immediately, spectacular, Coulagh Bay below the road, the Quay with fishing boats to the east, low-lying Eyeries Island and, beyond, the high mountains of Miskish and Knockgour. The road is all ups and downs. Illaunnameanla island, close to shore, is below us, a favourite of Harbour seals. A solitary electricity pole carries power to a navigation marker.

Our first stop is The Hag of Beara. "One of the oldest mythological beings associated with Ireland", the iron plaque at the gate says. The legend says this is the head of the pre-Christian goddess, An Cailleach Bhéarra, turned to stone as she waited for her lover, Mannanan Mac Lir, the sea god. The rock is time- and weather-worn. In some legends, the Cailleach was the goddess without whose endorsement a king could not be crowned; in others, she is the shaper of the landscape of bays and mountains. Visitors leave trinkets on the rock, coins, keyrings, shells; the appearance is that of a pattern tree. The plaque records her enmity with Saint Caitiaran who brought Christianity to the region, and a post-Christian legend says it was he who turned her to stone. The Hag of Beara are also figures in Scottish folklore.

We next stop at Kilcatherine, a 7th century monastic site possibly built by the monks that raised the stone beehive huts on Skelling Michael, 9 miles offshore. Texts differ as to whether Caitiaran was male or female; in some the saint is named Caitighearn, The Cat Goddess. An eroded gargoyle-like head – some say resembles a cat's face – protrudes at the end of a fluted neck over the roughly corbelled arched entrance to the ruin, now reduced to roofless gables with the eastern window of crude field stones beautifully made. One of the earliest stone crosses in Ireland stands below it. Ancient and modern graves surround the church, with many stylised Celtic crosses and old graves marked with stumps of stones.

We continue, enjoying magnificent vistas of Coulagh Bay and then, ignoring the road to Kilcatherine Point and, topping a rise silhouetted against the sky, come upon a breath-taking vista of Kenmare Bay (aka Kenmare River) with the misty blue mountains of Iveragh, mountains behind mountains, east to Coomcallee and Carrantouhil. The narrow road switchbacks through dips and rises, treeless highlands and wooded valleys.

Above Cleanderry Harbour, its mussel lines sheltered by islands, we turn right and are soon on the Beara walking route. Now, crossing moorland, we watch for a waymark on the left and a No Dogs Allowed sign opposite, and take a footworn track going right. After crossing a metal bridge, we follow the waymarks: the next is always visible from the last. This is moor and bog, with bog myrtle, bog cotton, reed grass and sphagnum. After a kilometer, we come in view of Lough Fada, the long lake. Here, at the eastern end, a stream flows out, reaching the sea at Cleanderry.

Our route takes us along the high ground, the lake on our right, reed beds between us and the water. This is thoroughly wild country, away from all habitation; only the waymark posts to connect us to the present time. At the end of the lake, we emerge on a narrow tarred road and, as we walk downhill to the trailhead, again enjoy vistas of Coulagh Bay and the Slieve Miskish mountains.

Herons, locally called Johnny or Julie-The-Bogs, stalk the shallows everywhere along these coasts. Elegant birds, they have recently been joined by Little Egrets, new additions to the birds of Ireland.

ARDGROOM WALK, CORK – KERRY BORDER

Distance: 10km, 2-3hrs.

Difficulty: Magnificent views, varied terrain. Byroads above the sea, one short, steep stretch, then a footworn track along a high ridge with panoramic vistas. Option to shorten or lengthen the route. Good boots advisable.

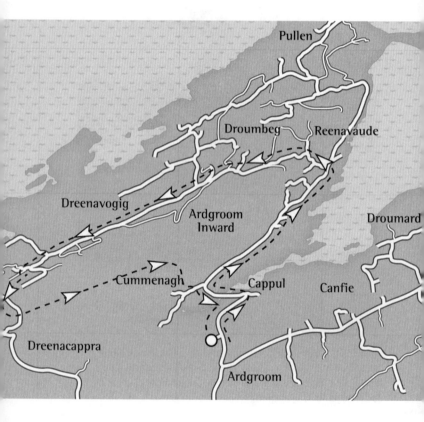

GETTING THERE:

Ardgroom is on the R571 Wild Atlantic Way Kenmare-Castletownbere road. In the village, take the L4911, signposted Beara Way and Pallas Pier, alongside Harringtons Grocery Delicatessen. We park nearby. (For alternative trailhead, see Paragraph 1 below)

THE WALK:

We continue on the L4911, crossing scenic Cappul Bridge at the head of Ardgroom Harbour. We are immediately in wild country, Tooreennamna and Tooth mountains behind us and the Iveragh mountains across Kenmare River, ahead. After 0.5km, we pass an unpaved roadway going left, with a yellow Beara Way waymark. We emerge here when we come down from the hills at the end of our circuit. We could make the nearby parking space our trailhead, shortening the walk by 2km.

We continue on the tarred road, the Beara Cycle Route, rough land on the left and tranquil Ardgroom harbour below us on the right. In July and August, the road verges seem on fire with swathes of orange montbretia in flower, and there are stands of purple loosestrife, pink Greater Willowherb, creamy meadowsweet and buddleia, blue or white. Across the Kenmare River, Sneem nestles beneath the range that rises to Carrantouhil, 1039m Ireland's highest peak.

We ask why huge Kenmare bay is called a river. The answer perhaps lies in its early Irish name, Inbhear Scéine, 'wild river mouth'; the Roughty and Sheen spate rivers enter it. Another version holds that an English milord who owned the bay shores wanted to assert fishing rights and dubbed it a river so that these would be granted or granted at less cost.

We turn sharp left, inland, at a handpainted sign for "Hekerthaus" and a Ring of Beara sign. Optionally, we may go straight ahead, making a wider round via Pallas Pier, used in mussel cultivation, and Bird Point pier, favoured by anglers, adding 3km before rejoining the Cycle Route.

Commercial groups produce organic mussels on Kenmare River. Not everyone is happy about this; the mussel ropes, suspended from lines of floating barrels, contradict the image of unspoiled Ireland, the deep bay with wild mountains on either sides; clearly, its natural glory is compromised. However, mussel farming provides a livelihood where the land is often unyielding.

A gentle climb takes us past patchy fields onto a mountain road. Now, the views over the bay are westward as far as Lamb's Head, below Caherdaniel, on Iveragh. On a long rockface, St. Patrick's Cabbage, a Lusitanian saxifrage, grows from moss high above the road. After a dog-leg turn, at a T-junction, we go left.

We must carefully watch out for Waymark 49, 200m along on the right. We take the track opposite, beside a No Dogs Allowed sign. After another 200m we see Waymark 50 ahead and now follow the yellow waymark posts, always visible ahead. Beyond post 52, stepping stones cross a wet lag, and a ladder stile climbs to a ridge above. Butterwort, an insectivorous pastel green rosette producing a violet flower, is common; also bog cotton, spike rush, cross-leaved heath, Irish dwarf gorse, and bog myrtle with red stems. Rocks are often beautifully patterned with lichens.

The 'top of the world' views are glorious — southward, the Caha range and north, across the bay, the backbone mountains of Iveragh, with Ardgroom village eastward below us. Small Heath and Grayling butterflies are common. We pass two ruined houses at post 56, bare stones and a single gable stark and emblematic against the backdrop of sea and the sweeping green peaks of Iveragh, another is almost subsumed by willow and bracken colonising what was once its home acre. After trekking 2km. across this paradise, we arrive, too soon, back at the unpaved roadway at Waymark 60, and turn right, back to our trailhead.

Prehistoric stone circles, standing stones, and stone alignments are everywhere in west Cork. Cork is said to have more prehistoric artifacts than any other county.

KERRY WILD ATLANTIC WAY WALKS FROM BUNAW TO SHANNON ESTUARY

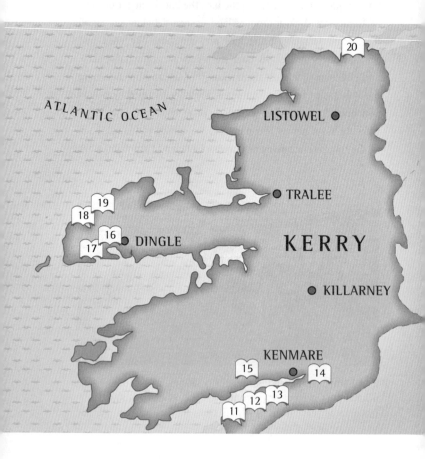

BUNAW PIER AND KILMAKILLOGE HARBOUR, BEARA WALK

Distance and Time: 10km. Allow 2hrs. minimum.

Difficulty: Small roads; some steep ascents and descents.
Magnificent scenery and photo opportunities.
Bring binoculars.

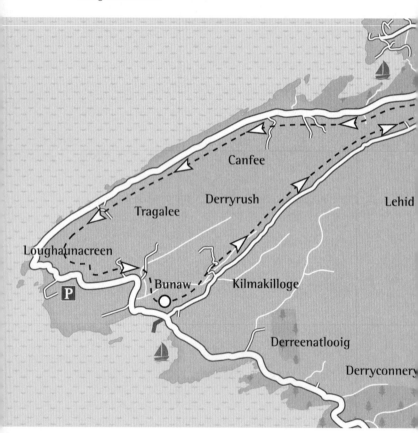

GETTING THERE:

After our previous walk venue, Ardgroom, and just before the village of Lauragh, the Wild Atlantic Way R571 coast road takes a spur to the left, the R573 — a brown sign indicates Kilmakilloge Harbour. We arrive at Bunaw Pier, with boats moored alongside, and Teddy O'Sullivan's pub opposite. The large car park is our trailhead.

THE WALK:

On fine summer days, folk sit at the tables outside Teddy O'Sullivan's pub at Bunaw pier and enjoy views of the harbour, boats and mussel lines, the Caha Mountains to the southwest, and Tooth and Tooreennamna mountains opposite. It is a colourful and lively scene.

The R573 Wild Atlantic Way continues past the pier. We set off on the road directly opposite the pier, between the car park and the quaint remains of an old cottage. We walk uphill; in spring and summer the ditches are ablaze with wildflowers, an outstanding feature of this walk. To the right, are fine oaks, like parkland trees, and spurs of the Cahas displaying classic examples of almost vertical folding. So verdant is the road that at times it is almost closed in by the exuberance of flora leaning from the ditches. Every common Irish wildflower is seen in its splendour, a pageant changing with the season.

The road climbs steadily and soon we are in hill country, trees and flowers replaced by gorse and heather, reedy fields with mountain sheep and bare rocks. We are "monarchs of all we survey" up here, the road little more than a track, no human settlement in view and uninterrupted vistas of Kilmakilloge Harbour, Droppa Mountain and other Caha peaks.

At 2km. from base, we come to a bird's eye view of the Kenmare River (a.k.a. Kenmare Bay) and, across it, the Iveragh Peninsula with mountains extending from the tip in the far west to the Macgillicuddy's Reeks eastward. The route then descends steeply, becoming verdant once more and arrives at a concrete bridge. Crossing it, we go left, and arrive at Lehid Bridge on the R573. We will go left here, but a short path, directly opposite, can take us through trees and over a pedestrian bridge to visit Lehid Harbour.

On the OS map the R571 and R573 between Kenmare and Lauragh are marked "Landsdowne Road". In 1841, the Marquis of Lansdowne, a Kenmare landowner conceived and part-funded the building of the bridge at Kenmare—Ireland's first suspension bridge — initiating the road running southwest down Beara's northern shore. It was replaced in 1932 by the present structure.

Our route going left at Lehid Bridge, is shaded by trees. When we last walked it — on a lovely weekend in August —there were few cars, but one should take sensible care. At gaps in the wildwood, we come in view of the bay, on our right all the way back to the trailhead. In August, the road is edged with long stretches of orange montbretia, purple loosestrife, creamy meadowsweet, and the ditches are draped with robust honeysuckle and white-flower bindweed. Often, the road runs immediately over the sea. We see the high mountains of Iveragh all the way west to Lamb's Head, and Rossmore, Rossdohan, Sherky and Garinish islands, and the Sneem River, on the opposite shore.

Now in view is the dramatic coastline ahead, Collorus Point and Dog's Point, and distant mountains, Slieve Miskish beyond the Cahas. We pass a small beach, and a Parking/Viewing place. The ruin of Kilmakilloge Church is on our right, with many old graves. The list of names of the interred are, all but a few of them local Irish names, O'Sullivans, O'Sheas, Healys, Sheenans. An old grave of McFinian Dhu notes that the family served "with distinction under the Austrian, French and Spanish flags".

Rounding the corner, we are back at our trailhead, and may enjoy a pleasant libation and repast at Teddy O'Sullivan's pub.

There are still wild goats in the Kerry Mountains.
From time immemorial Puck Fair is held in Killorglin,
Co. Kerry on August 12th. A wild, male goat is held for
three days on a caged throne high above the town
centre and crowned King of the Fair.

LEHID BRIDGE WALK, KENMARE

Distance: 6.5km, allow 1hr 40min. including sea shore visit.

Difficulty: The off-road section through a wood at the start, is easy going. The rest is on a small, quiet road. There are a few medium steep climbs, but no problem for a walker of average fitness.

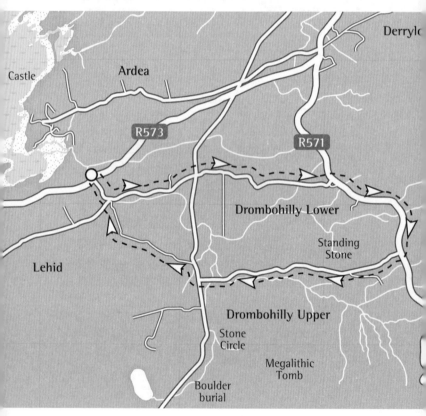

GETTING THERE:

We have taken the R573 spur of the Wild Atlantic Way, off the R571, to enjoy the Bunaw-Kilmakilloge walk. Now, driving along this coastal route, we reach Lehid Bridge, already mentioned on the Bunaw-Kilmakilloge walk. We stop here, parking under some trees on the left beyond the bridge, and set off on a new walk which takes us on a loop up the Lehid River.

THE WALK:

Lehid Bridge is stone-built, with a pretty mountain stream running beneath, a small waterfall upriver, gravel beds downriver. It is named Drombohilly, "bó" is the Irish for cow; the foaming water on its many small falls runs white as milk. At the time of writing, a sign prohibits salmon fishing because the river is being restocked.

Our walk takes us inland, upriver, but a short stroll downriver first will take us to the sea. We pass under fine oak trees, and across a narrow metal bridge, its floor of iron laths heavily corroded. Crossing it, we reach a path through oak woods, a worthwhile diversion leading to the shore and marvellous views of the Iveragh mountains on the other side. We will have these views from a higher prospect on our route after we retrace our steps to the R573, cross it and go inland on the road to the left of the river.

As we walk, we pass a concrete bridge on the right. The road is quiet, with grass at the centre. Hills are ahead, Knockreagh, with the Caha range running south. At 1km, we reach a crossroads and go straight through; the left would take us to Tousist hamlet. After a short sharp climb, we might pause to look behind us at the magnificent view of the Kenmare River (i.e. Kenmare Bay) with the backbone mountains of Iveragh. To our left, beyond a deep valley, we see the mountains behind Kenmare, as far as Mangerton and Carrantouhil in the Macgillicuddy's Reeks.

This is a winding, undulating road, with the rare farmhouse and no traffic. We descend steeply into a valley (2km from start) and reach the R571 signposted left Kenmare, right Castletownbere. We go right, picking up the Beara Way, and after 0.75km go right again just beyond a house with some pine trees. The road is unmarked but it is opposite an R571 sign and a telegraph post on the corner carries a handmade sign saying "Cheese" and a Walking Man waymark.

Falls on the Drombohilly River. We can see where the river gets its name which translates to English as "white as milk".

It's a narrow little road with great views of the Kenmare River and the mountains beyond, peaks to left and right and Knockatee peak ahead. This section of the Beara Way is called for Seán Ó Súilleabháin, whose initiatives led to many of the Beara Way and Kerry waymarked walks. Whortleberry shrubs proliferate on the ditches, called fraochán in Irish and traditionally gathered on the last Sunday of July and at Lughnasa, the start of the harvest festival. We look out for a Standing Stone in a field on the right, the site of large boulders and home to fine, strong curly-horned rams.

We now come to a T-junction, with signs, left, to Lady's Way and Beara Way and, right, to Kenmare's hospitality facilities. We have come 5km. from our trailhead. We shortly arrive at triple signposts and go left, on the Lady's Way route. Immediately after the turning, we pass a lane to a house lined by massive boulders laid on one another, like a Megalithic wall. A track opposite is lined by standing stones. All are most likely JCB created. We are now on an unmade road, going downhill, passing the occasional house.

We arrive at the concrete bridge we passed on the first leg of the walk, and cross it, turning left just beyond and retracing our steps, downhill now, to Lehid Bridge and the car.

A classic example of the quiet by-roads we follow in many of these walks, the high ditches near-vertical gardens of wildflowers, gorse, heather and fuchsia from February to October.

GLENINCHAQUIN WALK, BEARA PENINSULA

Distance and Time: About 7km, allow 2hrs.

Difficulty: Medium. Largely, shale-surfaced track. Some moderately steep stretches.

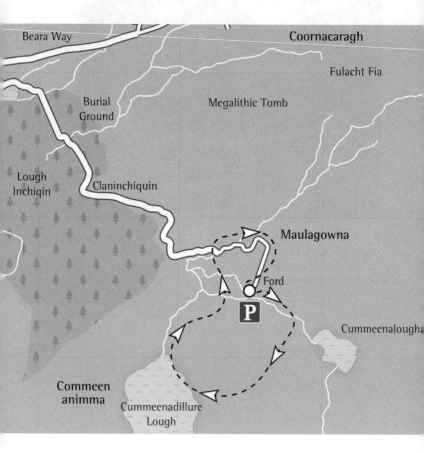

GETTING THERE:

Leaving Castletownbere and Eyries on the R571 Wild Atlantic Way, direction Kenmare, we are driving the north coast of Beara, the sea on our left. Some 12km. from Kenmare, a road sign on the right indicates Gleninchaquin Park. Go right. After 8km. the road ends at the second car park behind the Reception Centre. This is our trailhead.

THE WALK:

Parking at the second car park, we walk back to a green gate on our right and take the rough track climbing gently beyond. When the stream on our left is in spate, it rivals the waterfalls at the valley end, and is immediately beside us.

After the second gate, the path curves around and comes to a rustic bench. Behind us, we have the sound of falling water and, ahead, a panoramic vista of the Gleninchaquin lakes stretching down the valley with the distant peaks of Macgillicuddy's Reeks on the Iveragh Peninsula beyond. Kenmare bay, in between, is hidden by the contours of the land.

Our path now passes behind the waterfall, crossing the stream descending from Cumeenaloughaun tarn via a narrow iron bridge. We are now up high on the ridge at the 'horseshoe end' of the valley. As we start down towards the larger tarn or corrie lake of Cumeenadillure, the track of loose shale is verged by gorse and heather. The lake, cupped in a half-circle between the surrounding slopes, makes a perfect picture, the waters still and deep, so sheltered as to be almost unruffled even on windy days. A rough path leads down to its shores.

As we descend toward the reception area, the lone trees on the pasture below seem so shapely that they might be topiaried. From late spring onward, they stand in verdant glory and then, in autumn, when the leaves go yellow, we have the colours of our national flag laid out below us, green pasture, golden trees, with scatterings of white sheep in between.

So perfect are the trees, that I later asked Donal Corkery, the Park Administrator, if they had been lopped or pruned Not so, he told me; they were as nature had made them. Justly proud of the landscape which his family have owned and farmed for 130 years, he knows its geology, history and botany. The solitary trees were, he said, the few survivors of the oak forest that had once blanketed the glen but were felled for charcoal-making during the Industrial Revolution. Anywhere one turned a sod, one came upon ash, evidence of the charcoal burners. It was, of course a tragedy. But there remained small copses, stands of birch and alder, oak and aspen following the river along the lower valley, and old woodland still clinging to the steep mountainside across the lakes.

To the left of our shaley path, we see downy birch, with red bark and, on a hill beyond, a small, stone house with a thatched roof. A sign identifies it as a Heritage Site, with the restoration of a 19th century farm in progress. Visitors are welcome and a path leads to it, crossing a bridge over a stream issuing from the waterfall above. It is hard to believe that up to 1895, the little bothán housed a considerable family. We descend fairly steeply towards the green fields and reach a river fed by the twin falls running over the black, wet rock above as white as the famous milk of Kerry cows. Here, we may cross a bridge, or use the stepping stones.

A sign on the right indicates a path across the fields to the Reception Centre and car park. However, continuing on the track, we reach the road to our trailhead, enjoying various 'windows' between the trees which perfectly frame views of the waterfall across the pasture.

The sweeping green pastures, grazed by sheep and punctuated by perfectly-formed trees, spread beneath the twin waterfalls flowing down black rock from the tarns above.

KENMARE RIVER WALK

Distance and Time: 9km, 2-2.5hrs.

Difficulty: Very easy going, almost all the route is on quiet back roads. Lovely views of mountains, mountain streams and falls. A nice mix of wooded roads and open moor land.

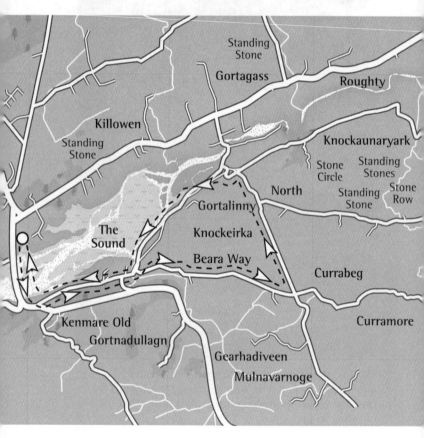

GETTING THERE:

We stop at Kenmare, a lively town at the head of the Kenmare River on the Wild Atlantic Way. The Post Office, our trailhead, is located at the southern side of town, before we cross the bridge.

THE WALK:

From the Post Office, we set off along the pavement towards the head of the Kenmare 'River' (actually the headwaters of the bay) and the bridge spanning it. St. Patrick's, a pretty Church of Ireland chapel, is on the left. We cross the bridge and then turn left off the N71, after the Riversdale House Hotel, taking the road signposted Sheen Falls and the Beara Way. The Kenmare River is on our left, unseen through the trees as we walk along this heavily wooded road.

We soon cross a pretty humpback bridge over the Sheen River. It has a fine parapet to lean on and there are some dramatic cascades to the left as it plunges down to the sea. Below, the big Kenmare River is almost millpond calm, absorbing this mad, dashing tributary with hardly a ripple.

The low hills at the start of the Iveragh Peninsula reflected on the Kenmare River below the town.

Immediately across the bridge, we turn right, following the Beara Way. This is a pleasant, country road. Heather thrives on the ditches; the left side supports typical Irish flora of the region, holly, gorse and bracken. Through trees on our right, we see an old woollen mill, an elegant, stone building, rising to three floors, with many windows. The nearby hills provide good grazing for sheep. After rounding a few corners, we hear the sound of rushing water and soon see rapids on the Sheen River on our right.

We continue, and pass a substantial old Kerry farmhouse with some fine ash trees and pines, a yew tree and a magnificent Scots pine. Shortly, we have views of the flanks of Currabeg hill and Curramore Mountain, with slabs of bare rock reflecting like mirrors when the sun strikes them after rain.

Reaching a 4-crossroads, we take the left turn (the Beara Way goes to the right). The road now is very straight, a typical 'bog road'. Soon, we start downhill, the mountains looming ahead; our view broadens to include all the range from Derrygariff to Knockbrack.

We come to another 4-cross roads; the road straight ahead, going down behind a farmhouse is an obvious shortcut to the bridge over the Roughty River, so we take that. Shortly, we reach a T-junction. We will soon be going left, on the Kilgarvan Cycle Route, but we divert right for a look at Roughty Bridge. A short distance along, we have a good view over a pleasant scene and the substantial stone bridge, with two arches. The Roughty River is the main 'feed' for the bay; it rises in the high land near Kilgarvan. Pearl-bearing mussels are found in some rivers flowing into the bay and are legally protected. Only one shell in a hundred contains a pearl, and only one in a hundred pearls is acceptable in size and clarity.

Now, as we walk south, there are acres of purple-headed reeds, moving like a sea in the wind, on the right hand side between us and the Kenmare River. The "river" here is wide, the fields that edge it are regularly flooded at spring tides. Through binoculars, one may see wading birds, curlews, redshanks, greenshanks and dunlin. Cormorants, various gull species and grey herons are also present.

The reed marshes end, and we see open water; in the early 2000s, new houses were built on the other side. We shortly find ourselves once more at Sheen Bridge. Then we are retracing our steps into Kenmare, westering home with, perhaps, the evening sun in our faces.

Mussel ropes, from which the shellfish grow, laid out on the tranquil waters of Kenmare Bay, the serried mountains of the spectacular MacGillycuddy's Reeks on Iveragh, behind.

BLACKWATER RIVER WALK

Distance and Time: 8km, 2hrs.

Difficulty: Easy going, on trafficless roads and bog track.

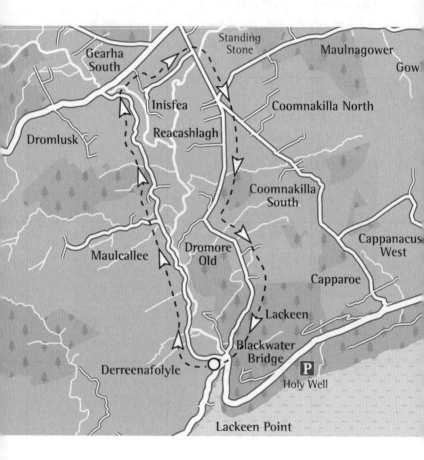

GETTING THERE:

We cross the bridge on the N70 Wild Atlantic Way between Kenmare and Sneem. In Kenmare town, the N70 is also signposted The Ring of Kerry. About 9km beyond Kenmare, we cross the narrow Blackwater Bridge at a sharp bend. Immediately after crossing the bridge, we park on the left verge. This is our trailhead.

THE WALK:

We have parked opposite the old Post Office, marked on the OS map. Before setting off, we should certainly retrace our steps to the Blackwater Bridge — we will be re-crossing it on our return, but viewing it before we start will make us aware, when we see the Blackwater River upstream, of how romantic and wild it is in this gorge. The double arched limestone bridge crossing the deep abyss was constructed in 1839, replaced an earlier bridge. To stand on the parapet and look straight down is a heady experience. The tall, narrow arches rise high over the dark river, broken into white water as it rushes over black rock far below. They support a roadway hardly wide enough for two cars to pass. Because of this constriction, and adding to its character, the parapets feature indented refuges on either side where pedestrians step in to avoid traffic. Built of local stone, the bridge fits appropriately into the natural environment; the bedrock over which the cataract runs is also limestone. Upriver and downriver, the steam flows calmly, hemmed by trees.

Returning to the Old Post Office, we take the road on the left side of it, the L7545, signposted Maulcalee. After a half kilometer, the Kerry Way veers off left, via a ladder stile. It is some 215km (134 miles) long, the longest of Ireland's National Waymarked Trails. We ignore the stile and continue up the quiet road ahead, flanked by silver birch, goat willow and holly, trees typical of Ireland's native flora; the tall gorse (French gorse) is, in fact, a deliberate import, naturalised here for centuries. The Blackwater is below us on the right, distinctly heard and often seen, with falls and rapids. A notice states that fishing is prohibited without licence. Knocknagullion, a rounded hill of 415m, rises on our left. A narrow anglers' path runs along the river bank.

As the vegetation thins, we see that the river is, here, a broad, dark, slow-moving stream, with shaded pools that, no doubt, offer refuge to salmon as they go upriver to spawn. We reach a neat hut on the left, apparently the "HQ" of the Kerry Blackwater Salmon Fishery. A wooden table and benches alongside offers an excellent picnic spot. The big rounded mountains to the west are Knocknagantee, Knockmoyle and Finnararagh, all not far short of 700m. Beyond them are Waterville and Portmagee.

The road now runs through bogland, with lower hills on the right. 2km. past the hut, we reach a T-junction and the R568, with a signpost, Sneem and Parknasilla left, Killarney right. We go right, crossing Gearha Bridge.

About 1km. along, we leave the road, taking an unsurfaced bog track down to the right. After 1km we arrive at a narrow, tarred byroad and go left. This quiet road takes us to another T, where we turn right, descend and cross a bridge over the pretty Derreendarra River. We are on the Ring of Kerry Cycle Route, and pass the Blackwater Tavern and Post Office, ignoring the two roads left.

The road runs through bogland and is typically straight. Low, reddish bog myrtle had colonised the wet ground. Soon, we come upon magnificent views of the Caha Mountains to the southwest beyond Kenmare Bay, which is hidden by the contours. The road is wooded as we head downhill, and soon reach the Blackwater Bridge and our trailhead.

Tall, slim arches bridge the Blackwater River, constructed from limestone in 1839. The road is only wide enough for one car to pass. The view to the river far below is dramatic.

DINGLE HARBOUR WALK

Distance and Time: 7km, 2.5hrs.

Difficulty: Pedestrian path, then field and cliff paths, and side roads on the return.

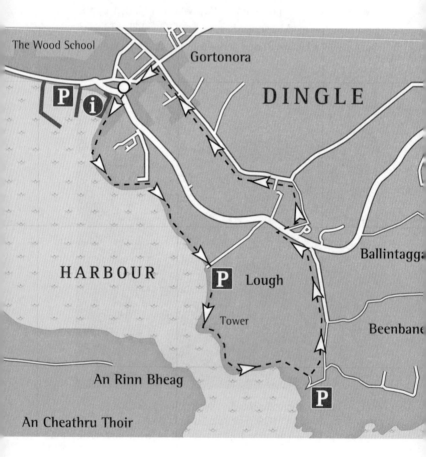

GETTING THERE:

Dingle, a feature town on the N86 Wild Atlantic Way, is called An Daingean in Irish and is recently famous for the its friendly dolphin, Fungi, who obliges vistors taking excursions on the harbour by cavorting within a few metres of the boat. Many photo opportunities! Entering the town, we park near Moran's Esso garage on the right, and walk down the lane opposite.

THE WALK:

We set off down the laneway opposite Moran's Garage. It is lined with small houses built in the 19th century by Lord Ventry to house fishermen he had evicted from An Rinn Bheag, a village across the harbour. He had decided to make the whole peninsula a private hunting estate.

At the end of the lane, we reach the sea and go left, on the made path along the shore. At low tide, when there is a narrow beach, one can walk along the sand. In summer, the Fungie-viewing boats pass close by and we can hear the whoops and gasps of the besotted dolphin watchers – indeed, we can see the obliging Fungie delight them with his repertoire of tricks.

Rounding the corner, we can see Hussey's Tower, a.k.a. Hussey's Folly, ahead. We reach a slim-persons' stile; after-dinner walkers of corpulent configuration may have to briefly take to the shoreline.

We cross a stream and reach Hussey's stone-built structure. The sobriquet 'folly' seems unkind: it was built not as a rich man's whim but as a charitable man's attempt to help the less fortunate, the victims of the Potato Famine of 1847. Hussey was a tenant of Lord Ventry, and saw the building of the tower as a way to provide the starving peasantry with employment.

Two small strands with rock pools adjoin the tower, lovely places for children to explore. A cutting through the low 'cliff' behind them ascends to a path passing along the field edges above us. Alternatively, we may return to the tower and climb to the field above it, where a stile beside a gate takes us to the cliff top path, between low hedges.

Dingle lighthouse is clearly visible, shining white on the promontory ahead. The cliff-side path affords us wide views of the open ocean. Walking on the slippery grass below the path should be avoided, threatening a fatal slide into the sea. A mile farther on, we come down onto the pretty strand of Bhinn Bhán.

Here, we reach a second car park and, now, head inland, making for the old road back to Dingle. Ignoring right turns, we continue due north. At the national road N86, we turn left and 150 yards along take the small road signposted Pax Guesthouse.

The byroad is gravelly, about wide enough for one car. A road joins from the right but we continue left (Marian Park). At this junction, the field on the right holds an impressive double-ring fort, almost 30 metres in diameter, the ground within raised higher than the land around.

Soon, we start to descend towards the town with its streets of tightly packed, coloured houses; the Kerry people, like those of west Cork, are fearless with paint. A gate in the ditch affords us a panoramic view from the harbour mouth all the way back to Mount Brandon.

We ignore any turns. Marian Park becomes Sráid Eoin, John's Street, with multicoloured houses on both sides. Reaching An Droichead Beag, we turn left onto The Mall, passing the Christian Brothers School with a beautiful garden ascending to a gable wall with a fine arched window. Passing a large tableau of the crucifixion, we reach the roundabout and go left to return to the trailhead. Many fine Dingle hostelries offer relaxing après walk fare.

A sturdy little trawler breasting the white horses on Dingle Bay. Dingle, also called Daingean Ui Chúis (The Fort of the Husseys) has been a fishing port for centuries.

VENTRY STRAND AND ST. COLMAN'S GRAVE WALK

Distance and Time: 7km, 2.5hrs.

Difficulty: A loop walk full of variety. Ventry strand and back roads, with a short stretch of field path. Sea shore and hills, legendary sites and medieval history and pre-history. Views of the distant mountains of Iveragh.

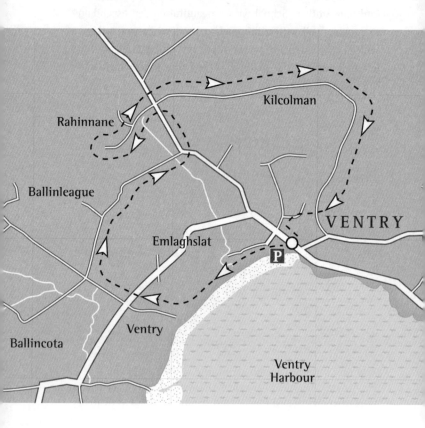

GETTING THERE:

We arrive at Ventry as we proceed west on the R559 section of the Wild Atlantic Way from Dingle. As we reach the town, we park near the Post Office, where we start the walk.

THE WALK:

From the Post Office, cross the R559 to a lane leading down to the sea. We reach Ventry Strand, legendary scene of the longest-lasting battle and mightiest victory of the Fianna, via a concrete walkway on our right. To the left is the Cliff of the Women, where legend says, the womenfolk of the Fianna warriors resided during the years of conflict.

At low tide, the beach is vast. In summer, we will find burnet and cinnabar moths in the dunes, banded snails, dune pansies and purple sea bindweed. In winter, Ringed plover, sanderlings and dunlin run along the tide line. Ventry harbour hosts a regatta, with currach races.

As the marram ends, we leave the beach via a cutting in the dunes. The sandy path becomes a narrow lane leading up to the church with the pub of the famous Kerry footballer Paidí Ó Sé opposite. We set off up the long, straight road towards the mountains - the rounded bulk of Mount Eagle, ahead to the left, and the pyramid of Cruach Mhárthain to the right.

At a four-cross-roads, we turn right along a bog road, with stands of reed mace and sedge in the wet fields alongside. The small fields on the hillside are divided by broad hedges. Above, the grey mountain shows bare rock in places.

Pausing at a bend in the straight road, we enjoy spectacular views across Ventry Harbour to the huge, blue hills of the Ring of Kerry. Now, for perhaps half a kilometre, we walk down an unbroken fuchsia lane where the buzz of bees and drone flies fills the air on sunny days.

At the junction, with a cluster of holiday cottages opposite, we turn left onto a larger road, ascending gently and come to a stone inscribed "Árd an Caisleáin" and a sign directing us left to Rathanane Castle. Although our route goes right, down the minor road opposite, the short diversion to see the castle ruins, across the fields, is worthwhile.

Seen from the lane, the ruin is stark, grey and roofless. Within the site itself, we appreciate the castle's true dimensions, built, as it was, on a more ancient double-walled ring fort. In the 15th century, the Fitzgeralds, Knights of Kerry, built a fortified tower house on the site this being their stronghold until it was taken by an Elizabethan force in 1602. Some fifty years later, again in Irish hands, it was destroyed by Cromwellian forces.

Returning to the main road, we cross it to take the bohreen opposite marked by a wooden Pilgrim's Route waymark, the yellow symbol of the Celtic Cross and a wayfaring saint. We now have breathtaking views of the sea, the big Iveragh mountains and the high cliffs at the end of the peninsula, albeit seen over the sprawling caravan park on Ventry Strand.

Nine miles beyond Iveragh's tip is Small Skelling, with the second largest gannet colony in these islands, and Skellig Michael, once the remote redoubt of saints and scholars. A Pilgrim's Route post indicates a field below us on the right in which the outline of a large monastic settlement is still clearly seen. Here, in the settlement of Kilcolman is the site of Saint

Colman's grave, and a stone carved with two Coptic crosses and an ogham inscription saying "Pray for Colmán the Pilgrim". Pilgrims following the Way of the Saints, Cosán na Naomh to the summit of Mount Brandon would have rested here.

In a wayside hamlet, a path ascending between the houses on the left continues the Pilgrim's Route and Dingle Way, crossing the peninsula. We stay on the road, now going downhill, the Skelligs straight ahead of us, salient on the western ocean.

Now, a sign carved in stone, "Mám an Óraigh" – the place of the springs – and then a quarry. Inside the gate, a track leads uphill to an impressive wedge tomb known locally as "The Munsterman's Bed". It may be necessary to seek landowners' permission to visit it.

As we catch sight of the caravan park and the beach, a waymark on our right directs us down a narrow track and, after passing through the ruins of a farmhouse, we reach a small road. Turning left, we walk down to the main road and about 100m further on reach the Post Office where we began.

Caherdongan, the remains of beehive huts, an ecclesiastical settlement, with the Three Sisters on Sybil Head facing the Atlantic beyond.

BALLYDAVID CLIFF WALK

Distance and Time: 10km. Allow 3hrs.

Difficulty: Easy going. The loop comprises a tarred road going north, and a cliff path on the way back, walking south. Especially scenic in late afternoon or early evening.

GETTING THERE:

Ballydavid vallage is on the Wild Atlantic Way (R549), just north of Murreagh.

BALLYDAVID CLIFF WALK:

Baile na nGall means "the foreigners' town", referring to a 9th century Viking settlement at Smerwick, a Norse name meaning "the butter harbour".

With the pier behind us, we set off, keeping left on the road, between houses. The road divides; we keep left. To the right is the truncated peak of Reenconnell. Tall, creamy meadowsweet swathes the verges in August.

We pass the mast of RTE Radio na Gaeltachta with a bungalow alongside it. In an area of traditional emigration, the RnaG studio provides a local living for Irish speakers.

The road is narrow, and difficult if there is heavy traffic, but this is rare. As we walk, Binn Diarmada, northern most of the Three Sisters headlands, sweeps gracefully skyward beyond the mouth of Smerwick Harbour. Sheep graze in the roadside fields. The stretch of road turning east towards the hills is especially colourful in August, the verges lined with purple fuchsia and orange montbretia.

With Mount Brandon straight ahead, we reach a T-junction and turn left. The land rises gently to low cliffs, northward. Some houses have a rick of black turf in the yard, like a miniature Gallarus oratory or an upturned black boat.

As the road descends, the sea is visible ahead. Binn Diarmada is to the left, Ballydavid Head to the right with Charraig Dhubh, (the black rock), offshore. We pass the Clifftop Restaurant, where a small path goes down to the sea. There is a sign for An Ghlaise Bheag village to the right.

We continue on the road, and turning down opposite The Old Pier restaurant we reach Dooneen Strand. Naomhógs lie by the road, their shiny black hulls turned skyward. Called currachs in Connemara, their Kerry name translates as "the small boats of the saints". It was from Brandon Creek, 5km north of here, that St Brendan the Navigator and his monks sailed west in a large, sailing naomhóg in the 6th century. Tim Severin crossed the Atlantic in a reproduction of their craft, thus proving that a Kerry man might well have navigated the coast.

After the pier, we return to the road and turn right, back the way we came, to the black-and-yellow road sign indicating a left curve. Our footpath begins behind it, a small sector of the beautiful Dingle Way.

This path along the clifftop is well worn. Here and there, big stones support luxuriant grey-green sea ivory, called Neptune's beard. Of an evening, we can watch the sun set behind the Three Sisters.

We cross heath land and pass a communications mast held erect by a web of steel cables. Ling heather and dwarf gorse flowers amongst the bedrock. On clear days, Skellig Michael, thirty miles south, is framed between the nearer Great Blasket island and the Iveragh mountains. As we approach more masts, Wine Strand is visible across the sea.

At an elbow of the path, sheep wire guards the cliff edge. Hereabouts, it is not unusual to see choughs, our glossy feathered, red-beaked crows, tumbling and diving overhead, raucous spirits of the western edge of Europe.

The path is eroded, and it is sensible to stay well in. After crossing a small stream, we pass a ruined World War II look-out hut and enjoy views of Dun an Óir. Skelling Michael and the Great Blasket float far off on the southern sea beyond.

Dun an Óir, a stronghold of the Anglo Normans Ferriters, was built on an ancient promontory fort. When a Papal force of 600 soldiers (Mangan's ". . . wine from the Royal pope will give you hope . . .") landed here in 1580 to support the Irish Catholic cause, the English bombarded them from land and sea until they surrendered, 'with honour'. However, all in the fort were then slaughtered, men, women and children. The poet, Edmund Spenser, and Sir Walter Raleigh were there and received tracts of Munster for their services.

The route now descends gently. In wild weather, the big rollers riding in to Mhuiríoch Strand run parallel to us as we walk. We shortly arrive back at Baile na nGall, where we began.

Scottish Blackface sheep. The mountains are theirs — and, apparently, the roads too!

GALLARUS AND KILMALKEDAR WALK: ANCIENT IRISH CHRISTIAN SITES

Distance and Time: 7km, 2.5hrs. including viewing.

Difficulty: Easy going. Pedestrian paths and side roads, beach.

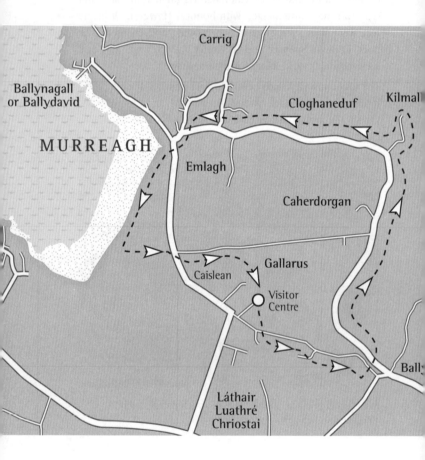

GETTING THERE:

The simplest way to reach the sites is on leaving Ballyferriter heading towards Dingle on the R559, turn left after 3km at the Smerwick Hotel, take the next turn to the right and Gallarus Visitors Centre is on the left. There is free parking and toilets here and this is where we start our walk.

Gallarus Oratory, constructed of unmortared stone in the form of an upturned boat. Built between the 6th and 9th centuries, it is still as dry as a bone inside.

THE WALK:

Setting out, we take the neatly gravelled path - signposted Gallarus Oratory - towards that unique stone structure created thirteen centuries ago. The design is inspired; perhaps the saint designed it. Light pours through a single shafted window in the gable. Nothing was used but stones, yet it is bone dry inside.

The hills rise behind, with stone walled fields, and houses scattered on the lower levels. On typical Atlantic days, the sun pierces the clouds like a giant searchlight sweeping across the hills, dark at one moment, dazzling green at the next.

At the tarred road, we go left, a narrow road, lined with fuchsia, climbing gently and, unfortunately, busy at times.

A stone plaque tells us we are in Baile na n-Ath. Opposite it, we take the unmade bohreen and go left at the road; it can be busy but we won't be on it for long. As it descends, the views of Smerwick Harbour and Wine Strand are magnificent.

Passing a long, straight road on the left, we continue to a stile and visit the Cathair Deargáin settlement, a well-preserved collection of five hut foundations within a ringfort, with a commanding position over the plain stretching to Murreagh Strand, present-day Ballydavid village, Wine Strand with Binn Diarmada rising beyond and Cruach Mhárthain and Mount Eagle to the south.

Kilmakedar Church, 12th century, the most important
ecclesiastical foundation on the Dingle Peninsula.

Looking right, we see other stone ruins, Tigh an tSeansailéara, the 13th century home of the Chancellor of Ardfert Diocese. The nearby church settlement of Kilmalkedar, built in the 12th century and the most important ecclesiastical foundation on the Dingle peninsula, is described as an "Irish Romanesque cathedral in miniature".

An ancient hand-sculpted cross at the church settlement of Kilmakedar. It has stood here in all weathers for nine hundred years.

Kilmalkedar was also a centre of learning. Within the church is a 7th century abcedarium stone, carved with the earliest surviving Roman lettering in Ireland. There is also a holed stone, indicating earlier pagan worship, and an ogham-marked stone outside. Nearby is a crude stone cross, dramatic in simplicity and resilience, a relic of Celtic Christianity, the faith before the Roman frills. Similar crosses stand at the monastic settlement on Skellig Michael, seven miles out to sea.

Back on the lane, we take the sign for the Pilgrim's Way on the right, the route of the old Saint's Road to the summit of Mount Brandon for the pilgrimages to St Brendan's shrine. Below it, is the small St Brendan's well, still visited by the devout on Easter Day.

Reaching the road, we go right, descending gently, the sea ahead. Soon, a narrow path to the right takes us to the enclosure of Argail Bréannain, Brendan's Oratory, which predates Gallarus. Further along, we see the steeple of the Church of Ireland, built in 1860 and now deconsecrated.

We pass the village of An Mhuiríoch and continue onto Murreagh Strand, host to many birds in winter. In summer, the rock pools teem with life.

We walk left along the beach - Dun an Óir and Cruach Mhárthain are landmarks in the distance ahead. The path up from the beach is sandy before we cross a field and, at a farmyard, follow the sign for the Way of the Saints. We come out to a farm with a castle on our right, a 16th century, Fitzgerald stronghold. The trailhead at Gallarus is only a few minutes down the path.

CARRIG ISLAND AND THE SOUTH SHANNON ESTUARY SHORE, KERRY

Distance and Time: 8km, 1.5-2hrs.

Difficulty: A there-and-back walk, level, on pavements, marked road verges and saltmarsh tracks.

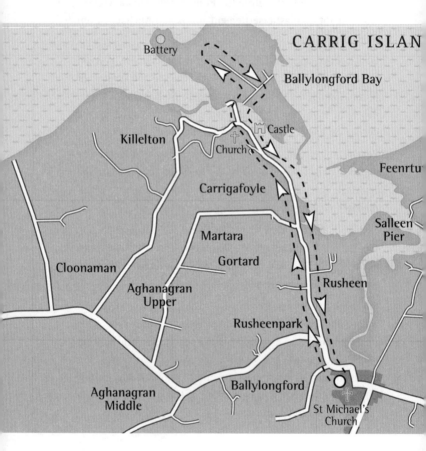

GETTING THERE:

On the Wild Atlantic Way north of Ballybunion, we take a short spur to the left, the L6010 signposted Carrigafoyle Castle, immediately before the village of Ballylongford. Crossing the bridge over the tidal Ballyline river, following signs for the Coastal Drive, we park at St. Michael's Church, our trailhead. The extensive car park and church grounds are superbly furnished with information plaques relating the history of this storied region.

THE WALK:

Leaving the car, we follow the waymark opposite the church gate. The pavement takes us along Quay Street. Afterwards, a white line divides the verge from traffic and after 200m. we reach a junction with an impressive Scots pine and take the quiet road signposted Carrig Island and Carrigafoyle Castle, 2km. We pass Aghavallen Church, in ruins, on the right; Kitchener of Khartoum was baptised there in 1850. Lislaughtin Friary, one of Ireland's great abbeys, is just NE of the town.

Depending on the time of day and the light, the views across the broad Shannon are crystal clear or shrouded in river mist. In misty conditions, Carrigafoyle Castle, perched on the shore ahead, reinforces the romantic illusion. Stone tools were recently discovered in the castle's proximity. Neolithic groups foraged here, possibly even Mesolithic hunter-gatherers as early as 8,000BC.

We shortly see water to our right, and saltmarsh, and on the opposite side of the estuary, the tall chimneys of coal-burning Money Point, the largest power station in Ireland. The SW tip of Carrig Island comes into view, often with beach anglers on the shore. Wading birds stalk the muddy shallows. Overhead cables carry decals, to make them visible to overflying birds. We see the castle, solid and impressive, to the right of the road about a kilometre ahead.

Gorse and rough grass colonises the island; a derelict dwelling and telegraph poles are the only visible artefacts. At the castle, notice boards in the small car park tell us that it is open from June to September. An excellent illustration of the castle under siege in 1580 shows the original layout of the buildings, and the position of the cannons shelling it from the high ground above the road to the left, where a medieval church in ruins may be seen. A ship in the estuary bombarded it from the north.

Considered the strongest fortified Irish tower house of its era, Carrigafoyle was built by the O'Connors. In 1580, a force of seventy Irish and Spaniards held it for the Earl of Desmond for three days until explosive cannon demolished the front wall of the upper storeys of the five storey structure. Defenders who survived were hanged and all booty seized was sent to Queen Elizabeth. In the restoration work, the breach in the front wall was left open, an inspired decision, allowing full view of the interior, its room spaces, windows and stone corbels that supported the floors. A well-preserved spiral staircase of 104 steps climbs 27m meters to the battlements, looking across to Scattery Island near the Clare shore, its round tower and church ruins.

Carrigafoyle Castle, built by the O'Connors in 1580.
The front was blown out by English canon during the
Desmond Rebellion, and the defenders, Irish and
Spanish, were hanged.

Leaving the castle, we cross the causeway to the island. At the T junction, signs give information about beach fishing to east and west. We walk west along a rough path towards the large, rectangular blockhouse about 1km ahead, one of six estuary batteries installed by the English after 1798, fearing a French invasion. The sunken interior – reached at one's own risk! – comprises circular spaces making perfect sun-traps, sheltered from the wind. A derelict house stands nearby. We have views of Beal Point, the long sand beach at Bunaclugga Bay and the Clare shore all the way to the open ocean.

Our return route to the trailhead offers interesting fresh perspectives on the castle and town.

Bramble flower on a wayside hedge. The flowers come in white and in pink. In August and September, the hedgerows on byroads are often laden with plump, delicious blackberries.

CLARE WILD ATLANTIC WAY KILRUSH TO BALLYVAGHAN

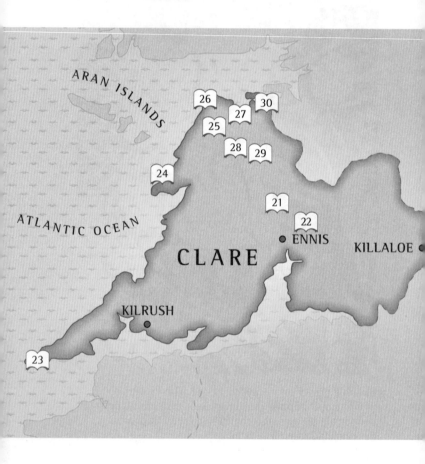

DROMORE WOOD LOOP

Distance and Time: 6km, about 2hrs.

Difficulty: Wooded tracks, lanes, lakeshore. Easy walk, no ascents.

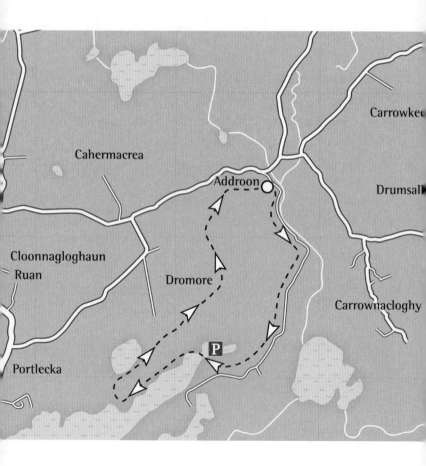

GETTING THERE:

A visit to Dromore Woods, part of the Burren National Park, is an interesting and worthwhile diversion from the largely coastal experience of the Wild Atlantic Way. We can reach the woods, a Nature Reserve, from Kilrush on the Wild Atlantic Way and, if we fancy, and especially if it happens to be June 23rd, we can then visit Spancilhill only 15km away across the M18, and see one of Ireland's oldest and biggest horse fairs.

Afterwards, we can return to the Wild Atlantic Way at Kilrush and take the Loop Head coastal route, or cut across country through Ennistymon and Lahinch and pick up the Wild Atlantic Way there. making our next walk the Cliffs of Moher.

The Dromore Woods reserve is a stronghold of the Pine Marten, an animal that recurs in old Irish texts but was persecuted until recently in the belief that it preyed on the eggs and chicks of game birds. It does do this, but is not a threat to their conservation. Now that it is again installed in the list of protected Irish fauna, it has emerged that this apex predator is a natural control against the incursions of the North American grey squirrel which has eliminated the native Irish red squirrel in many areas.

At Kilrush, turn off the Wild Atlantic Way on the N68 to Ennis and then take the R458 to Crusheen. At Crusheen, a narrow road to the left (direction Ruan, but not signposted) takes us to signs for the Mid-Clare Way. Following this, we cross a small stone bridge over the River Fergus, and go left for Dromore Wood entrance.

THE WALK:

We park outside the gates near the grassy triangle with picnic table and benches created from large stone slabs. The itinerary described on the Shannon Region Trails website begins at a car park at the lake shore, some 2 km. inside the reserve. On an especially sunny summer weekend, it may be better to use the reserve car parks, but for most of the year parking outside will be no problem and we can enter the wonderful world of the reserve on foot, not having already seen half of our itinerary from the car.

Arriving in Clare, a county famous for music, prehistoric stone artifacts, the karst limestone pavements of the Burren and its rare flora and fauna.

Dromore Woods and Nature Reserve are managed by the Forest and Wildlife Service and extend over almost 1,000 acres of woodlands and lakes.

As we set off down the driveway, the River Fergus, here no more that 10m to 15m wide, runs alongside us on the left, sometimes behind a screen of willows. The Fergus rises in the Burren and flows through seven lakes before reaching its tidal stretch at Ennis. It is famous for its brown trout; the limestone riverbed provides ideal spawning grounds and habitat.

We pass signboards on the right, mapping the many trails through the reserve. We will be walking the entire circuit, marked in purple. On either side of the driveway, is mixed forest, almost wildwood, the trees spindly and crowded. At about 1km along, on a path into the woods on the right, we can take a brief diversion from the drive. The path emerges after approx. 400m. and we continue on the tarmac.

As a break in the woodland and a white bridge comes into view ahead, we can enter the car park on the left, where there is a bench looking out over the lake, a tranquil spot where, if there is a stir of wind, one can, indeed, hear the legendary "lake water lapping with low sounds by the shore". The feathery heads of the reeds, on their long stems, are beautiful against the water, even in winter when they are brown and even tattered. The tallest grasses in these islands, the tough, stiff stems make excellent thatching material.

Coming back onto the driveway, we now enter a car park on the other side, and cross it to follow a wooden boardwalk, very much like a bridge. The lake bird most likely to attract our attention is the Great Crested Grebe, especially if we are walking in springtime, when both sexes develop beautiful dark head plumes which they erect during the elaborate courting display. In the 19th century, a fashion for these feathers, to decorate lady's hats (sometime, the entire plumage was worn) almost led to their extinction in these islands. The courtship rituals involve much diving, acrobatic neck-convoluting, and rising breast-to-breast out of the water offering one another gifts of water plants. In June and July, the chicks may be seen riding on the parents' backs. In winter plumage, the white face and necks of the birds are conspicuous.

Beyond the boardwalk, we reach a 16th century O'Brien castle. A robust ruin, it has interesting features within but the only doorway, arched in limestone, is closed off with a stout metal gate. Above it, is a fine piece of medieval stone carving that reads, "This castle was built by Teige, second son to Connor, third Earle of Thomond and by Slaney O'Brien, wife to the said Teige Anno D". In my photograph, I see that part of the lovely name, Slaney, is gone altogether. Once a spacious tower house with a fine lake view, its location would have owed as much to defence as to aesthetics; having water on three sides would have been an advantage in the turbulent years of the Confederate Wars. The O'Briens occupied the castle until 1689; it fell to ruin in the hundred years that followed.

Continuing ahead, on the Castle Walk, we pass Dromore Lough and then the oval-shaped Lough Garr. Dromore holds bream, roach, tench and perch, and fishing is permitted.

Our pathway continues through woodland to our trailhead at the entrance gate.

A townland on the Spancilhill walk, following this one, is called Obriencastle, named for the tower house illustrated here. Tower houses were built in Ireland, Scotland, England and the Basque Country in the early Middle Ages.

SPANCILHILL AND O'BRIEN LAKES LOOP, EAST CLARE WALK

Distance and Time: 8km, 2hrs.

Difficulty: An easy walk, following the Mid-Clare Way along quiet back roads.

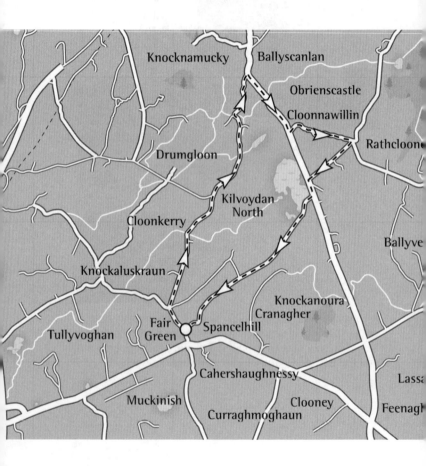

GETTING THERE:

If we happen to be passing along the Wild Atlantic Way on June 23rd., a diversion will provide a chance to witness and walk through the bustling world of a unique, old-fashioned Irish Horse Fair. Irish Travellers and their families will be there in force, bargains struck, hands spat on and slapped to seal the deal. Highly recommended by this writer.

From Kilrush, on the Wild Atlantic Way, we take the N68 to Ennis. The Cross of Spancil Hill is 5 km east of Ennis on the R352 regional road to Tulla.

THE WALK:

"Last night as I lay dreaming of pleasant days gone by/ Me mind being bent on rambling to Ireland I did fly/ I stepped on board a vision and I followed with a will/ Till next I came to anchor at the cross at Spancil Hill."

The day my wife and I walked this circuit, the winter hedges were still leafless, but the holly and ivy, winking like silver dollars when the sun shone, brightened our way. Redwing thrushes flew from the bushes, wild Russian or Scandinavian migrants, mad as the mist and the snow of the lands whence they came. The narrow roads were trafficless and the gently undulating countryside would be glorious in spring and summer. A man told that the O'Brien lakes held "coarse" fish, but fish being "coarse" seemed hard to reconcile.

The route was easy, waymarked and signposted, doubling back at the first right turn. About 1km later, we went left on an even smaller road, overlooked by a ruined O'Brien castle on a rise. At the next junction, going sharp right, we left the

Mid-Clare Way for 300m, before rejoining it above O'Brien's Big Lough, and following it back to Spancilhill.

As we walked I regaled my patient wife with tales of the day when, forty years before and fresh home in Ireland for the first visit in a decade, I had gone first to Doolin for the music, and then to Spancilhill for the 23rd of June Fair, the oldest horse-fair in Ireland, as I was assured by the many ready historians I met in the pub in the late afternoon.

When I arrived at Spancilhill at eleven that morning, I "stepped aboard a vision" indeed. It was as good a June day as one could hope for, the sun already hot in the sky. The Fair Green at Spancil Cross was a kaleidoscope of colour, horses everywhere, roans, chestnuts, blacks and bays, skewbalds, piebalds and dappled greys, horses as huge as Clydesdales and tiny as Shetlands and Connemaras, shaggy horses and svelte horses, and amongst them, roaming in all directions, the visitors and the long-time aficionados of the fair.

There were farmers and travellers and bloodstock fanciers, shapely girls on ponies with riding hats, men in cloth caps and baseball caps and cowboy hats, and all the noise and fun of the fair. Motor homes, caravans and marquees lined the periphery, beer tents, chip tents and tea tents, and hucksters stalls and tackle vendors. And there was music, street singers and Sean Nós singers, buskers, box-players, fiddlers and bodhrán beaters, tin-whistle-smiths and one-man-bands.

Spancil Hill, the song, was written by Michael Considine in 1870 in California, where he died aged 23. It relates the dreams of a homesick emigrant during the Gold Rush, and his return, in a dream, to the people at home, all now grey-haired, and to the girl who was once his love. It ends with the lines, Then the cock, he crew in the morning,/ He crew both loud and shrill,/ And I woke in California,/ Many miles from Spancil Hill.

A 'spancil' is a tether used for hobbling horses or cattle. Once, when horses hauled the rolling stock of imperial armies, buyers came from all over Europe to this East Clare village and the horse fair was the largest in Ireland.

The lakes loop is a fine walk on a winter day, but even better in spring or summer. And best of all, when one can take in Spancil Fair, on the 23rd of June.

In a scene that might have been taken from a painting by Cuyps (1620-1691), cattle cool off in a roadside river on a hot summer's day.

LOOP HEAD WALK

Distance and Time: 2kms,1hr.
(Extended Loop: 4–5hrs. 15kms.)
Difficulty: Easy, a short walk along a cliff top path. Take care in windy weather. The route can be extended to a longer, more challenging walk.

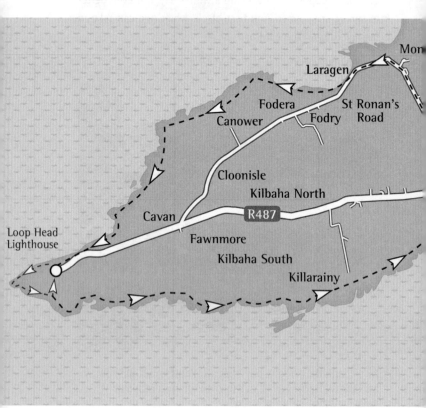

GETTING THERE:

From the town of Kilkee, we take the R487 (Wild Atlantic Way) west for 28km to reach the tip of Loop Head, and the lighthouse car park. We park and set off from here.

THE WALK:

With the open Atlantic to the west and the Shannon estuary to the south, Loop Head is a long narrow strip of land, jutting westwards into the ocean. This peninsula has long been visited for its outstanding natural beauty, and was voted the best holiday destination in Ireland in 2013.

Setting off from the car park, we walk north to reach the cliff top path, and left along the headland with the lighthouse on our left. These undisturbed and remote cliffs are an important refuge for a wide range of seabirds. Guillemots and kittiwakes nest here, and the peninsula is used as a resting place for migrating birds heading south for the winter. Rarities are often recorded here, possibly attracted by the lighthouse at night in bad weather conditions, and American vagrants are regularly blown across the Atlantic by hurricanes when migrating from North America to South America, crossing the Caribbean. On a clear day, dolphins and even whales can be seen out at sea; the mouth of the Shannon is home to approximately two hundred bottle nose dolphins, the largest group in Europe.

The sheer outcrop jutting into the sea on our right is Diarmuid and Gráinne's rock, named after an epic love triangle tale from Irish mythology. Gráinne, betrothed to the elderly Fionn Mac Cumhaill, elopes with a young warrior, Diarmuid, and the pair are pursued by Fionn for many years. All across the country there are caves, trees and other refuges named after the errant couple.

The small cairn visible on top of the rock is not an ancient monument, but was erected by death-defying rock climbers in more modern times.

On our left, we soon come to the foot of a huge sign, marking out the word 'Éire' in white stones arranged on the grass. During World War II, long before GPS, these signs were constructed all along the western coast, indicating to airmen that they were safely over neutral Ireland. There is also a look-out post nearby, where soldiers were posted to observe and report all military operations off the Irish coast. There are over 80 similar outposts positioned in strategic locations along this coastline.

As we round the tip of the headland, we keep an eye out for a nearly hidden path through a narrow cleft to a precarious, south facing ledge. Here, Henry Keane, a local landlord in the 19th century, had the inspired idea of planting flower gardens perched 60 metres above the roaring Atlantic. Standing (or picnicking on a fine day) on this exposed shelf, one can only marvel at the eccentricity and indomitable enthusiasm of the Victorians.

There has been a lighthouse on this headland since 1670, when a signal fire was lit each night on the roof of the lighthouse keeper's cottage. The modern tower is open to the public as an information and exhibition centre from April 3rd to October 2nd. From the balcony, on a clear day, one can see as far as the Aran Islands to the north, and the Blasket Islands to the south. After taking in the lighthouse, we continue down the southern coast of the headland for a few hundred metres, before turning left again towards the road and the car park.

Those who wish to extend this walk can continue along the southern coast of the peninsula as far as The Lighthouse Inn at Kilbaha Strand. Here, we take a left turning directly beside the pub that cuts across the peninsula to the northern side, where we can again go left to follow the coastline back to the car park. This extends our walk to 15km (4-5 hours).

Loop Head, County Clare.

CLIFFS OF MOHER WALK, CO. CLARE

Distance and Time: Doolin to Hag's Head and return to Visitor Centre for bus, 15km, 3-4hrs.

Difficulty: Moderate. Unwise in wild weather.

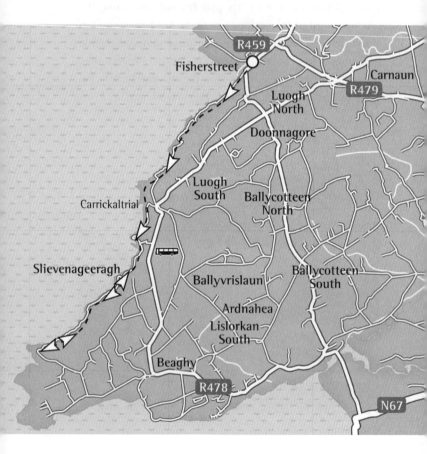

GETTING THERE:

Spring and summer is the time for this walk and Doolin, on the Wild Atlantic Way R479, is the place to start. In Doolin village, we park on Fisher Street and start walking south on The Burren Way. Ahead, we enjoy 6km. of undeveloped wildness, dramatic cliffs, seabirds and wild flowers before we come upon the Visitor Centre and camera-carrying visitors from all over the globe, a sight worth seeing. Beyond this – a 30 minute stretch of Liscannor stone-laid walkway between O'Brien's Tower and South Platform – we again find ourselves relatively alone above the steep, romantic cliffs at Moher Tower and beyond.

The path ends just beyond Hag's Head. We retrace our steps to the Visitor's Centre (with cafes and interesting information displays). If we wish, we can take a bus back to Doolin; at the time of writing, there are four buses each day.

THE WALK:

After leaving Doolin, we arrive at a fork, the left leg signposted the Cliffs of Moher. We ignore this, and head right, for the gate, continuing on The Burren Way. A sign board explaining the distances, the terrain, the challenges of the rough trail and the risk of rough weather.

About 1km away, beside the road going left and climbing the hill, we see a round, fairytale-like castle. Called Doonagore Castle, a tower house built by an O'Connor chieftan in the 14th century, the name is unfortunate but appropriate. In 1588, 170 Spanish survivors of an Armada ship wrecked nearby were hanged there by the High Sheriff of Clare, appointed by the English crown.

Our path follows the coast, rising and falling with the topography, at times nearer or farther from the clifftops. There is a great feeling of space, the sky and the ocean, empty but for the Aran Islands on the near horizon. Stiff-winged fulmar glide past us, riding the updrafts. Outcrops of primroses, birdfoot trefoil, kidney vetch, scurvy grass and sea pinks are like mantles blown by the wind onto the cliffs' shoulders.

The highest cliffs, 214m, are just north of O'Brien's Castle which we see upon rounding Aillenasharragh headland. Sir Cornelius O'Brien had it built in 1835, apparently to impress female visitors. Galway Bay, the islands and the Connemara mountains can be seen from the parapets.

Around O'Brien's Castle, and as we leave it, we encounter visitors on all but the most inclement days. Below the path on the cliff side is a large rock platform, now fenced off; years ago, foolhardy souls would walk to the very edge, or lie flat on their bellies to peer over. Beneath it is a stark sea stack and Goat Island, a ridge of rock topped by scutch grass and sea pinks. There and on nearby cliff ledges, niches and shaly slopes countless seabirds nest. Curtains of guillemots and razorbills sweep back and forth like large swifts, hard to see against the dark rock faces without binoculars. Some 30,000 birds from 29 species inhabit the cliffs. Watching them, one forgets the crowds.

We now leave the Burren Way and soon the stone path becomes an earthen track. Moher Tower is silhouetted on the farthest headland, probably built by the British to watch for Napoleonic fleets after the invasion attempt of 1796. Below it, and the WWII look-out nearby, we see small, wave-beaten coves. The tower provides nesting crevices for choughs, a glossy black crow with red legs and beak, and shelter for walkers in bad weather. Returning to the Visitor's Centre for the bus back to Doolin, we enjoy dramatic views of the O'Brien's Castle, and of the Aran islands on the near horizon.

A sea stack off the cliffs of Moher, site of a thousand sea birds' nest in springtime.

SLIEVE ELVA WALK

Distance and Time: 9.5kms, 3-3.5hrs.

Difficulty: Easy, a casual walk along gravel and paved roads with some low stone walls to be traversed.

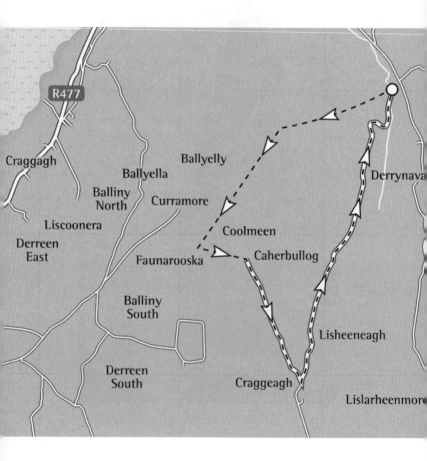

GETTING THERE:

Between Doolin and Ballyvaghan, on the R477 (Wild Atlantic Way) lies the village of Fanore. At the northern end of the village is a turning to the right on to the L5047; the church of St Patrick is signposted. Take this road and head inland for 3.2km to reach a Y junction where we take the road to the right. After 200m we see a gravel track on our right. We park and set off from here.

THE WALK:

We strike off uphill on the green road before us, which we will follow for about 3kms. To either side there are meadows, rich with the unique fauna of this region. The Burren is famous for its magnificent selection of birds and animals, and this walk gives one a perfect opportunity to explore and enjoy them.

The area is home to over 1,100 species of plants, and is the only place in Europe where one can find Mediterranean and Alpine species living side by side. Most of this region has been designated a Special Area of Conservation, which helps to protect its unique biodiversity. Some easily spotted animals are the feral goats (of which there are over a thousand), hares, rabbits and foxes, but Ireland's rarest animals are also to be found here, amongst them pine martens and slow worms.

Pine martens, a predator not dissimilar to a Irish stoat but twice the size, are rare in Ireland, and at one point were believed to have only one stronghold, here in the Burren. However, recent surveys have shown that their numbers are rising and that they are spreading out across the country since they have been given conservation status. They were persecuted as vermin previously.

Slow worms, a legless lizard resembling a small snake, are not native to Ireland, and are believed to have been released here in the last fifty years or so, with the Burren being the only place that they have ever been recorded. In Britain, where they are native, they have been granted a protected status as their numbers have been rapidly diminishing in recent years.

As we ascend we soon leave behind any trees or bushes that have managed to survive in the open Burren karst terrain. The karst platforms give the area its name; 'an boireann' means 'the great rock' in Gaelic. Here in the 'grikes' or fissures between the slabs, wild flowers and grasses proliferate. This road we are walking is part of an old network of roads across the Burren, once the main routes for the people and livestock.

Approaching the brow of the hill we reach a Y junction and keep left, following an arrow marker. The track soon levels out and we have expansive views of the surrounding hills with the Aran Islands off to our right. At 344m Slieve Elva (Sliabh Eilbhe) is the highest point of the Burren; on a clear day we can see the mountains of Connemara to the north.

We pass through some iron gates, taking care to shut them securely after us. Soon afterwards the road begins to descend gently, and here we keep an eye out for another arrow marker. We DO NOT follow this marker, but come off our green road onto a smaller, rougher path to our left. We follow this path along the northern edge of Sliabh Eilbhe and soon come across a black and white cross marking a holy well, the Tobar an Athair Calbach. Following the track around to the right, we pass a patch of spruce forest. Soon afterwards, we pass through a gate to a farmyard, which we cross to reach the tarred road. Here, we turn left.

Shortly, we reach a break in the wall which leads us across the field to Poll na gColm, an impressive cave and one of the entrances to the longest cave system in Ireland. At over 12km long, this labyrinth is a favourite among intrepid potholers. Following this quiet road downhill, we gradually emerge from the limestone landscape to the greener edges of the Caher River valley. After a number of bends, the river itself becomes visible nearby on our right, and we are back at our trailhead.

Low weathered hills relieve the flat limestone pavements of the Burren.

BLACK HEAD LOOP WALK

Distance and Time: 14kms, 4.5hrs.

Difficulty: Hard, a challenging walk with some stone walls to be crossed. Be aware of the deep crevices on the karst landscape.

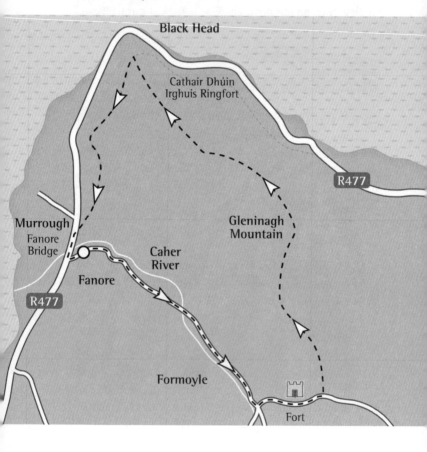

GETTING THERE:

Between Doolin and Ballyvaghan, on the R477 (Wild Atlantic Way) lie the village and beach of Fanore. At the northern end of the village, the church of St Patrick is signposted, 150m inland on a side road (L5047). We park and set off from there.

THE WALK:

With our backs to the church, we turn right and head up this byroad, named by local wits 'the Khyber Pass'. As we follow this ascent, the bubbling Caher river is rushing downhill past us on our left. Here, in this small valley, rocky fields stretch out on either side of the road, punctuated only by an occasional wind-sculpted tree or bush, bravely withstanding whatever the vagaries of the weather, often quite wild on this coast. As we continue, the valley deepens and the sides steepen, and we clearly see how the river cuts its way through the landscape.

After about 3.5kms we reach a junction with a road marked for the 'Burren Way' heading off to our right. We ignore this, and 100 yards further along take a gravel road to our left, uphill. We climb the winding track and are rewarded, when we reach this first summit, by the arrival at the ruined remains of Cathair an Aird Rhois. This is the first of the ruined forts which we will come across. Just past the fort, we cut through the wide gap in the stone wall on our left and strike out across open ground, starting as grassland but soon turning to limestone karst pavement. We aim for the mound ahead of us, the summit of Gleninagh Mountain, crossing several stone walls along the way.

From the pillar at the summit, we head for the next summit to the northwest, keeping to the saddle. Take care here as there are fissures and cracks in the rock which are sometimes difficult to see, and skirt carefully around any small drops that you may come across. The next summit, called 'Dobhach Brainín', is marked by a cairn, thought to be of prehistoric origin. From here we enjoy spectacular views over the Atlantic with the Aran Islands laid out directly to the west.

Descend from this summit to the northwest, carefully traversing a number of small terraces. Here we come across the impressive ruins of the Cathair Dhúin Irghuis or the fort of Irghuis. This is thought to be up to 4,000 years old, and may once have been the seat of a Celtic King. It stands in a breathtaking location on this barren plateau, overlooking the wide and empty ocean below it. This location was chosen, presumably, for the reason that an attacking enemy could be seen approaching for miles.

We continue downhill until we join a green road bordered by stone walls, and turn left. We follow this for about 2.5km, before meeting the first houses. Numerous stone walls cross this green road. On either side are patches of grass and wild plants, soon changing to bare, stony fields. Here we have the opportunity to see some of the rare and unexpected flora of the Burren, where Meditteranean, Arctic and Alpine plants live side by side due to a combination of the unusual climate and unique landscape.

The temperatures are suprisingly mild, with average air temperatures between 6 and 15 degrees Celsius. The absence of frost and a very long growing season allow a large variety of plants to thrive, and over 75% of the plants found in Ireland are represented here. Amongst them are many of Ireland's rarest species, including the emblematic Spring Gentian, an Alpine flower, and 24 other species of orchid, a delight to behold when flowering in late spring and summer. We begin to see houses and soon the track turns to gravel. We turn left on to the paved road, and follow it for 300 metres (care should be taken as this is a main road) before turning left again to reach our trailhead.

Walls of sharp, fractured rock divide land over which cattle roam on the limestone pavements of the Burren.

BALLYVAGHAN, THE BURREN WALK

Distance and Time: 8km, 2 hrs.

Difficulty: No steep climbs. Green tracks and quiet by-roads.

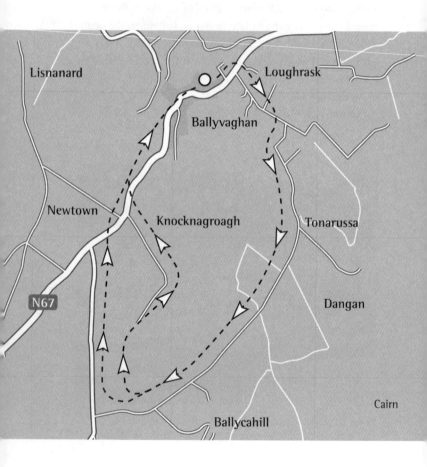

GETTING THERE:

Arriving in Ballyvaghan on the R477 Wild Atlantic Way from Fanore direction, we go left at the T-junction on the N67 Kinvara road. Our trailhead is the car park behind the Spar supermarket farther up the village on the left.

Despite the crowds of visitors that flock to this most famous of Burren Portal Tombs, the site has not lost its magic or its majesty. One could reach it by compass bearing, crossing the moonscape, limestone pavement, as my wife and I did years ago, but there may be issues of trespass and, as it is within 100m of the R480 in any case, one cannot pretend that this approach will imbue it with the sense of isolation in a pristine landscape.

THE WALK:

Leaving the car park, we walk 200m on the N67 in the Galway direction and take the second turn right, L5036, signposted Lough Rask. As we walk between houses, there is a small cemetery on the left, almost hidden by trees. Cowslips grow amongst the old headstones in springtime. Soon the dramatic stone-scape of the Burren comes into view, and we see how bright green fields lap the very margins of the bare limestone on the hillsides.

A laneway on the left takes us to Lough Rask, passing through a stone stile beside a green gate. The lake is weedy, and brackish, with sparse bird life, mainly mallard. However, the trodden path around its perimeter is a pleasant diversion, very much a 'wild' walk, with willows, meadow grasses and wild flowers.

Retracing our steps to the top of the lane, we turn left and then take the first right; "Waterstone Cottage" is painted on a stone on the verge. We pass Dolmen Lodge and Waterstone Cottage. Just beyond an old farmyard with overgrown gardens, we reach two gates and pass through onto a green laneway bordered by stone walls. Stone walls divide the stony fields, dotted with orchids and cowslips in spring and summer. Westward, the hill of Cappanawalla rises, part pasture but much rock. Cattle are wintered on such uplands in the old Burren 'winterage' tradition, with cattle allowed to wander the hills.

After moonscapes of limestone and grykes, passing through a stile at the end of this lane, we come to a gravelled road. Ahead, cattle graze in green fields and, beyond a gate, is a large, barn-like structure, with antennae. We go right, along the dead straight, gravelled road. Behind us, we have glimpses of Galway Bay and the distant Connemara mountains; in the middle distance, the slim steeple of Ballyvaghan church. Spots of bright yellow lichen on the stone walls, outcrops of brilliant yellow gorse and the white flowers of dwarf blackthorn break the grey monotony of the limestone. High limestone cliffs rise to our left. Rock roses and stunted ash and willow are typical here, holly and hazel in profusion. I was surprised to find white, garlic-smelling ramsons on the verge, usually a plant of old forests.

In a field on the right, with a solitary tree, a ring fort is clearly discernible on a slight salient, suitably overgrown with sceacs (blackthorn), holly and hazel, all suitably old, 'magic' Irish trees. The fields just afterwards are bounded by boulder walls, rather than stone walls, made possible by new 'magic' JCBs.

We pass Aillwee Mountain and the entrance to Aillwee Cave, and reach a tarred road.

After a tarred stretch, and then a potholed stretch, we can take a path (1) across stone fields as marked in the OS Map in square 2205. After 500m, this meets a lane taking us to N67, where we turn right. Alternatively, (2) we can continue on the road, and turn right at the T-junction onto the R480 and right again onto the N67 to take us back to the village and the trailhead.

In County Clare, there's no shortage of places to go or signposts to show you the way.

POULNABRONE & CAHERCONNELL STONE FORT, BURREN WALK

Distance and Time: 6km, 1.5hrs.

Difficulty: Easy going; no steep hills.

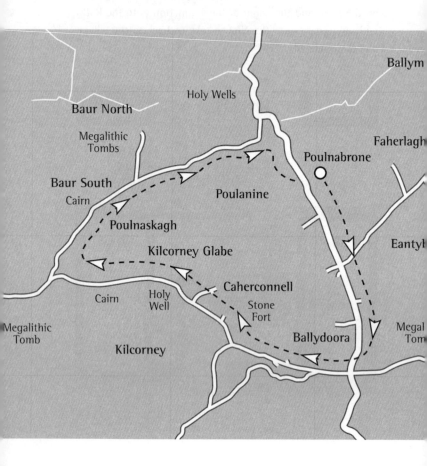

GETTING THERE:

We may proceed to Poulnabrone from Ballyvaghan village on the Wild Atlantic Way with or without taking in the Burren 'introductory' walk starting at Ballyvaghan village, as related previously.

Despite the crowds of visitors that flock to this most famous of Burren Portal Tombs, the site has not lost its magic or its majesty. One could reach it by compass bearing, crossing the moonscape, limestone pavement as my wife and I did years ago but there may be issues of trespass, and as it is within 100m of the R480 in any case, one cannot pretend that this approach will imbue it with the sense of isolation in a pristine landscape.

From Ballyvaghan, we first take the N67 and, after about 1.5km at a wide junction, we take the R480 and after approx. 6km. we reach Paulnabrone Dolmen.

THE WALK:

It is true that its timelessness – a monument constructed of stones old beyond imagining, arranged by a people who dwelt in millennia past – is best appreciated at dawn or sunset, when crowds are not there to remind us of Time Present. Seen from aspects where the road, fences, pathways, interpretation boards and ropes are not in view – only the limestone plains stretching away beyond, and the sky above – one can perhaps imagine a world where man was so small as to be almost insignificant but, already advanced in his understanding of the heavens and the trajectories of stars, was beginning to make his mark and leave his testimony as in this monument here before us.

A dominating feature on the Burren skyline, excavations in the 1980s found the remains of some 16 to 22 adults and 6 children buried beneath it, along with a polished stone axe, some weapons, quartz and bone jewelry, and pottery. It likely remained a sacred site long after the Neolithic period of its foundation.

After parking at the car park, we set off left onto the R480 which, for nine months of the year is uncrowded. It is straight, there is excellent visibility and traffic tends to move at a leisurely pace. The other roads we join are prefect for walking.

The emblematic dolmen, Poulnabrone. Excavations revealed that it was an ancient burial place and a hoard of weapons and jewelry was also found beneath it.

After 800m we reach the entrance to Caherconnell Stone Fort. This uniquely well-preserved ring fort built between 400 and 1,200 AD, is circular, 80m in diameter with walls 2m thick and up to 3m high. Developed for tourism, stone paths lead to it. It has been extensively excavated in recent years. It is open from mid-March to October.

Leaving Caherconnell, we again go left on the R480 and 1km later reach the waymarked Burren Way at Ballydoora Crossroads, where we go right, downhill. After 200m, at a bungalow, a minor road goes left, uphill. From it, Poulawack Cairn is visible on the hilltop to the south. We continue right and soon can see limestone cliffs ahead. The large pond on our left is possibly a turlough. The scenery southward is exceptionally lovely. The landscape on all sides is replete with cairns, tombs, souterrains: we need only look at the OS map to find them. Burren artefacts, being stone-built, survive, and the area has experienced less changes than other parts of Ireland.

Nearer the limestone cliffs, we pass the ruins of an ancient church on the left, one gable standing, with a graveyard around it. A kilometre farther along, we take the road going right, almost doubling back on ourselves, an extremely quiet, narrow road. Hazel woods lie below us to left and right. The landscape is now very flat, supporting large cattle. As we start to descend a slope, we have extensive view of stone pavement ahead. Descending, we round some corners, and at the T-junction go right on the R480 to the Poulnabrone car park, our trailhead.

CARRAN TURLOUGH
LOOP OFF WALK

Distance and Time: 7km, 1.5-2hrs.

Difficulty: Easy going; no climbs.

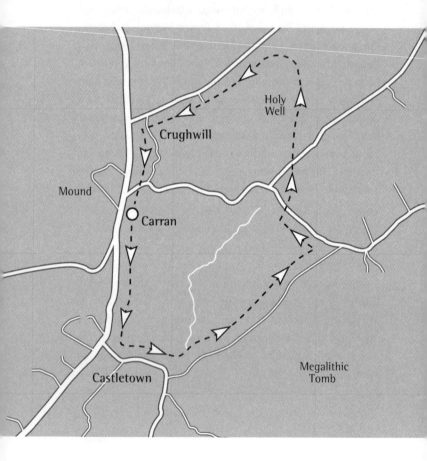

GETTING THERE:

After visiting Poulnabrone, we can take a route back to the Wild Atlantic Way via the interesting Carron Turlough or Polje, the largest karst depression in northwest Europe. A loop walk on quiet roads circles this large hollow which, when rainfall is high and groundwater wells up through underground springs, is filled, very quickly, with a seasonal lake (Carron Turlough). As the season dries, it empties just as quickly, the water draining underground through subterranean channels and swallow holes.

To get there, we go south from Poulnabrone on the R480, and after 1km we reach Ballydoora Cross. We turn left and pass through Meggagh, reaching Carran village after approx. 3.5km. After our walk, we can return to the Wild Atlantic Way by going north on the L1014 and L1016 to Bell Harbour, about 10km.

THE WALK:

Our trailhead is at Cassidy's Bar at the T-junction where we meet the L1014. Starting with our backs to the bar, we set off to our left, away from the village, passing the turning uphill to our right and following a signpost for the Michael Cusack centre. Cusack, the founder of the GAA, was born in Carran parish in 1847.

As we proceed, views of Carran Turlough open up to our left. This is one of the largest turloughs, or seasonal lakes, in Ireland, with an area of 150 hectares. Turloughs are a feature of karst landscapes, and almost unique to Ireland; the only other example is in Wales. In autumn these hollows flood to form shallow lakes, and do not dry out again until May or even July. Some may even flood and drain in a matter of days, depending on rainfall. Our walk takes us around the full circumference of the lake.

After 750m we turn left onto a smaller road. The turlough is now visible off to our left, with the low hills of Slievecarran behind it. We follow this winding lane for 500m before coming to the ruins of a small castle in the field on our left. Fifty metres later we reach a junction where we turn left, joining part of the Burren Way.

The Burren Way follows a lane at this point. The trees on the left soon become sparser, affording us closer views of the turlough across the fields. As we continue along this straight route, we come to the shores of the lake — its very existence depends, of course, on the season, and its depth depends upon amount of local rainfall. The flora of turloughs is of great interest to botanists, as it comprises distinct zones or layers marking out the changing water level. The result is noticeable bands of certain plant species, dependant upon the extent to which they can survive periods of drought and flooding. Water birds, including Whooper swans, teal and widgeon frequent the turlough when the flora provides good feeding.

As we proceed along this lakeside lane, the landscape becomes more barren and karstic; bare rock, punctuated by patches of grass, stretches out on both sides of the road. Our trailhead is visible across the turlough to our left. In Summer, when the lake has dried out, only the small Castletown River runs through the middle of this large hollow. The lake fills with water from springs at its northern end, and this water eventually drains through a sinkhole, disappearing back into the ground. After 1.5kms we meet a T- junction. Here we turn left again, still following the waymarks for the Burren Way.

Butterwort, a carnivorous plant found in wet places. Its sticky leaves attract and trap insects, which are gradually digested by the plant.

On this road we pass a ruined farmhouse on our left and some 700m farther on, we arrive at a junction. The Carran Field Research Facility is a couple of hundred metres to the left, a centre established by the National University of Ireland Galway for research at Carran Turlough and at the Burren area in general. We do not pass the facility but, instead, turn right, following signs for the Burren Perfumery. We then go left almost immediately, through a gate and onto a grassy track, following the signs to Templecronan Church, just a couple of hundred metres cross-country.

This small ruin of Templecronan Church, nestled in a hollow in this dramatic landscape, is steeped in history. The site of a 12th century monastic oratory, it is believed that there were much earlier buildings on this site and there may have been a pagan temple in antiquity. Several carved stone heads, of humans and animals, protrude from the walls, and there is evidence that these were moved from their original locations, suggesting they were part of earlier structures. Near the church, the remains of a large high cross are visible, as is a holy well, possibly also predating Christianity. Two ancient shrines nearby were once important pilgrimage destinations. One, called St Cronan's Bed, is said to hold the bones of St Cronan.

From Templecronan we continue in the direction we were walking, and soon join a small back road. Turning left onto this, we head downhill, with stone walls on either side. After a kilometre, we reach a bigger road and turn left, back towards Carran village. We pass the national school and the church, and then walk about 250m uphill along the pavement to the trailhead.

Fuchsia, a native to South America, forms corridors
of scarlet and purple flowers along the bohreens and
lanes of Munster.

ABBEY HILL WALK

Distance and Time: 6.5kms, 2hrs.

Difficulty: Moderate walk along green roads and across karst limestone landscape, and a moderate climb to Abbey Hill. Take care in windy weather.

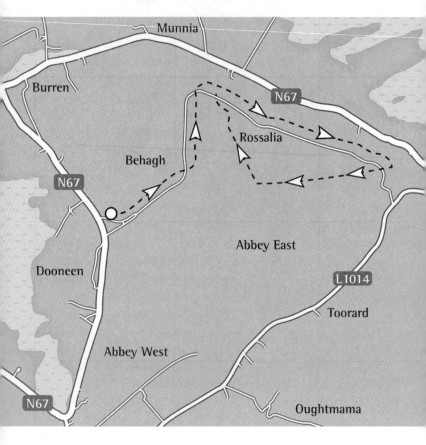

GETTING THERE:

From the town of Ballyvaghan we take the R67 (Wild Atlantic Way) north towards Kinvara. After 9km we come to the church of St Patrick on our right. We park in the large car park and set off from here.

THE WALK:

We set off up the narrow road between the church and the car park, with the sea at our backs. This tree lined, tarred road soon turns to gravel and opens out into views of the barren Burren landscape above us to the right. The contrast between the lush agricultural pasture and the vast hard tracts of stone is particularly evident here, with only a low stone wall acting as a border to separate them. We head straight on, climbing gently.

The road swings around to the left and we are now, ourselves, bordered by the traditional stone walls of the Burren, the stones splashed with patches of white and yellow lichens. There are several hundred species of lichen to be found in the Burren, some of which are very rare and have only survived here due to the lack of disturbance by man. The walls served a dual purpose in this region, to delineate holdings of land, and to clear the fields of stones. On our left we have wide views over Poulnaclough Bay with Mouneen Mountain behind. Trees are few and far between here, and those that have managed to grow do so at sheer angles, bent inland by the prevailing winds. It has recently been proven that pine and hazel trees once proliferated on this landscape, prior to the advent of humans. Traces of charcoal, found by archaeologists in the area, show that the patches of trees were cleared to make space for agriculture and livestock from as early as the Neolithic Age. It was previously assumed that the Burren's unique 'empty' terrain was formed when glaciers scraped all soil and vegetation away during the last ice age but, in fact, trees did manage to take hold again, until they were cleared by our ancestors about 2,500 years ago

As we come to a bungalow on our left, the views open up in front over the Aughinish Bay and the Dooras Peninsula, with Galway Bay in the distance behind. The road levels out here, skirting the edge of the hill, its imposing bulk rising steeply to our right. After just over a kilometre, we come to a small stone pillar on our right, and behind it, about fifty yards from the road, is St Patrick's Well. Here clean, fresh, limestone-filtered water pours from a small metal spout. The Abbey referred to in the hill's name is Cormocroe Abbey, at the base of the southern slope. Although not reached by this walk, it is visible from near the summit. This 13th century Cistercian Abbey is adorned with beautifully carved pieces of the limestone from the local landscape and well worth of a visit.

The road begins to turn right, and here we need to find a small gap in the wall to our left through which we pass. We then follow the path uphill, which soon turns from boggy meadow, to rock. Shortly, the cairn which marks the top of Abbey Hill comes into sight. Now we climb across the classic karst terrain, taking care to avoid the deep fissures. We reach the cairn at the summit, 240m above sea level. From here, the views are panoramic and one feels that the ascent has been well worthwhile. Black Head is to the west, Galway to our north and Oughtmama and Turlough Hill stretch off to the south.

Having enjoyed these views we set off again, keeping the wall on our left, and follow it all the way down the hill as it curves around to the right. Near the base of the hill we find a break in the wall and pass through this. From here we descend to the track below, the unmade, green road where we started out. We turn left to return to the trailhead.

Cormocroe Abbey, one of the great medieval abbeys of Ireland, seen in the distance from Abbey Hill. Well worth a closer look before we leave Clare and continue into Galway on the lovely Wild Atlantic Way.